Love and Commitment

Carol Leavenworth is director of the Career Center, Colorado College. She has been active in the field of psychology since 1970 and is the author of three books previously published by Prentice-Hall.

For Jo, Sally, Barb, Loa, and Susan

Ah Love! Could you and I with him conspire
To grasp this sorry scheme of things entire
Would not we shatter it to bits—and then
Remold it nearer to the Heart's Desire!

Rubaiyat of Omar Khayyam

CAROL LEAVENWORTH

Love and Commitment

YOU DON'T HAVE TO SETTLE FOR LESS

A SPECTRUM BOOK

Prentice-Hall, Inc., Englewood Cliffs, NJ 07632

Library of Congress Cataloging in Publication Data

Leavenworth, Carol.
Love and commitment.

(A Spectrum Book)
Includes index.
1. Love. 2. Commitment (Psychology) 3. Inter-
personal relations. I. Title.
HQ734.L372 306.8'7 81–2236
ISBN 0–13–540971–3 AACR2
ISBN 0–13–540963–2 (pbk.)

Quote facing title page is from Rubaiyat of Omar Khayyam,
trans. Edward Fitzgerald (New York: Random House, 1947).

A SPECTRUM BOOK

Printed in the United States of America

10 9 8 7 6 5 4 3 2 1

This Spectrum Book can be made available
to businesses and organizations at a special discount
when ordered in large quantities. For more information, contact:
Prentice-Hall, Inc., General Book Marketing,
Special Sales Division, Englewood Cliffs, New Jersey 07632.

Prentice-Hall International, Inc., *London*
Prentice-Hall of Australia Pty., Limited, *Sydney*
Prentice-Hall of Canada, Ltd., *Toronto*
Prentice-Hall of India Private, Limited, *New Delhi*
Prentice-Hall of Japan, Inc., *Tokyo*
Prentice-Hall of Southeast Asia Pte., Ltd., *Singapore*
Whitehall Books, Limited, *Wellington, New Zealand*

Contents

vii

Preface

For as long as I can remember I have been enchanted by love stories, both in literature and in real life. My childhood fascination with fairy tales led me to believe that the quest for one's prince or princess must be the great romantic adventure of a lifetime. Living happily ever after, bathed in the warmth of shared love, seemed to me to be life's ultimate experience.

As I grew older it became apparent that the romantic myths I had absorbed were not often reflected in real-life experience. My relationships with college boys were either boring or uncomfortably unstable. Divorce was becoming commonplace, and many of the relationships of my married friends were visibly unhappy. Even the optimism of youth could not overcome the sensation of impending disappointment.

I began reading commentaries on love written by older, wiser, and more experienced thinkers. They assured me that the passion and excitement of new love does not and should not last. As lovers grow closer, they move to a new level of love: a deeper, more contented, and more mature kind of

loving. This, the sages said, is the goal of a true adult relationship.

An honest look at my own deepest wishes revealed a
longing for both the rapture of new love and the stability
of a lifelong commitment. My observations indicated that
what passed as contentment in many relationships seemed
more like boredom and thinly disguised dissatisfaction. I
thought perhaps that as I matured I would see things more
clearly. But as time passed and my desires remained unchanged, I began to suspect that the answers lay in another
direction. Wise people had been wrong before, so perhaps
the current wisdom about love might be wrong as well. Although what I saw around me, combined with the advice of
my elders, made the inquiry look like a discouraging waste
of time, I decided to see if there were not some way of resolving
this seemingly irreconcilable paradox in my desires.

Ten years of research and both clinical and personal experience have followed this decision. In the process I have learned
that my apparently conflicting desires are shared by many,
and perhaps shared by most of us. I learned from my clients
that desires often reflect undeveloped potentials, and I hypoth-
esized that if this is true in some areas of life, it may well
be true in love, too. Slowly I gathered information about how
people prevent themselves from feeling and being the way
they wish to be. As I began to put this knowledge to work
in my own life and to assist my clients in doing the same, I
discovered that we can resolve our inner and interpersonal
conflicts in ways that do give us an opportunity to experience
more of love's passionate excitement in our long-term relationships.

This book is the result of my work thus far. Like any
book, it can only point out possibilities and suggest pathways
that the reader may follow. Real changes will take place in
readers' lives when there is a strong commitment to a creative
application of the principles discussed here in real situations.
Sometimes this will not be easy. If it were, we would have

all solved our relationship problems long ago. But for people whose heart's desire is to have more love and less pain in their lives, this book will help in making a beginning. As we all learn to love more freely and fully, new books will be written to take us even further down the path to becoming ever more loving people.

Many books written today seem to require a word or two about language. I have attempted to avoid sex role stereotyping in the language used here while at the same time describing real situations. Since most of us are still caught up in our sex roles to one extent or another, and since our language tends to lag behind our ideals, some of my attempts have been more successful than others. Additionally, I have used the words *spouse, mate,* and *partner* interchangeably to describe people involved in a dyadic, intimate, and primary relationship. Although these words tend to imply a legal marriage relationship, the ideas apply to any alliance in which the individuals are committed to building a long-term intimate connection with one another.

It seems to me that love is like the glue that holds us and our world together. Recent social trends reveal that a stronger application of this adhesive is necessary if we are to solve the many personal, social, economic, and political problems that confront us. A lot of people still settle for a "good enough" relationship. Many even settle for a bad one in preference to no relationship at all. We have, however, reached a point in human evolution where it is possible for a great many of us to have wonderful relationships. And, by learning to meet our own needs for vital and fulfilling intimacy, we may also be learning the skills that will aid us in solving some other problems, too. If you listen to your deepest heart and you truly do desire to have more love in your life, you can. You don't have to settle for less.

My thanks to Susanne Ritchey and Barbara MacDougald, fellow researchers in the laboratory of life; to Gay Hendricks, always a stimulating and beloved companion and collaborator; to Sarah Stewart, Jeff Livesay, and Judi Leavenworth for their comments and help; to Lynne Lumsden and her staff for bringing my words to you.

CAROL LEAVENWORTH
Colorado Springs, Colorado

Love and Commitment

1

The Mystery of
Relationships

The Southern Oregon seacoast holds a special fascination for me. High cliffs and monolithic boulders dominate the vistas. It is a scene that is never at rest, one filled with unceasing conflict and turmoil. Great waves crash against the rock, are tossed back, and then relentlessly return. There is a wild beauty here and great force and energy. The force of wind and wave is almost flamboyantly obvious, yet the rock in its resistance has its own more subtle force. Imperceptively, as the rock yields to the wave and is eroded, new structures are being built. Despite all the noisy activity, the very profound changes taking place here occur very slowly and quietly.

There is much to be learned in this place, for the relationship between sea and shore has many similarities to relationships among people. We enter each others' lives with our own unique kind of energy, complimentary yet different in thrust and focus. Where our energy meets little resistance we flow smoothly along our chosen path like a wave on a broad beach. But where there is conflict between our thrust and another's, the resulting resistance can create noisy encounters and violent emotions. The greater the energy expended in thrust and resistance, the louder and more active the by-products may be. Beneath all the furor that sometimes seems to be leading nowhere, profound changes are taking place. New patterns are developed, often very different from those intended by either party. In the process, new opportunities, like new sea channels, are constantly emerging and then passing, inviting us to discover creative and unexpected directions for our energy.

Sometimes the most devastating conflicts lead to the most amazing and creative changes in the direction of one's life. The discovery of a spouse's affair can result in a stronger marriage based on more mutual understanding and acceptance. A child's failure in school or defiance at home can force a family to examine their relationships and learn more loving ways of being together.

At age thirty-five Dr. Sherry Manning became president of Colorado Women's College. The college was in serious financial difficulty at that time. The summer before she took over the presidency there had been only twelve applicants for admission to the fall freshman class. But Sherry Manning had learned from her own experience that the worst problems can lead to the most creative solutions. She saw that the situation at Colorado Women's College presented an opportunity to create a unique educational environment for women, and she was ready to accept the challenge.

At twenty-one Sherry was married and working as a salesperson for IBM. "My ambition at that time was to become a branch manager at IBM," she recalls. "That's all I could imagine for myself then. I didn't want to be a vice president—that was out of my range. I had no notion of doing anything but staying on my floor in that building on that street in Baltimore, Maryland."

But circumstances intervened in Sherry's life. Her husband was sent to Colorado to fulfill his military commitment and Sherry went with him expecting that she would easily be able to find another job. When her job search proved unsuccessful, Sherry found herself at loose ends for the first time in her life. "At first I was miserable. I didn't know why, but my feelings about my life had changed. I knew I had to get a sense of excitement back into my life."

Sherry started her own business and decided to take some graduate courses at the University of Colorado. "I signed up as a PhD candidate even though I had no interest in getting a doctorate, because I knew the PhD students had the first choice in registering for classes." Without knowing it, Sherry had taken the first step toward a whole new career in the field of education. From then on, she began to notice how every barrier she confronted seemed to open a new door to an unexpected opportunity. The birth of her first child helped her to decide to pursue her PhD in earnest. An uncongenial job environment caused her to focus more of her energy into writing and consulting activities. Soon she was building an international reputation and gaining the experiences that would qualify her to become one of the youngest college presidents in the country.

When President Manning assesses the course of her career so far, she concludes, "My life is much richer and more colorful than it would have been if I had stayed at IBM. It's a diverse life and while it doesn't always go smoothly, it fulfills me.

"I'm more tempered now than I would have been if I had been able to single-mindedly pursue the career I first imagined for myself. And I'm a better president because of that."

The sea and the land are joined eternally in their relationship. Every channel that can be explored, every structure that can be built or destroyed in this relationship will be, because there is no escape either from the conflict or the creativity. Human relationships are more vulnerable, partly because of our greatest gift, the freedom of choice. This is as it should be. People are more complex and therefore more fragile structures than rock, sand, and water. Our survival depends on our ability to build more than we destroy in our lives. Our happiness depends on how much more energy we can expend in the building activities than in destructive ones.

People are more than simply products of nature; we *are* nature in its most potent creative manifestation. The patterns of energy we create in our relationships with one another and with the world around us are major contributors to the unfolding of creation. We have seen how our own misuse of the environment has caused the extinction of entire animal species and led to the pollution of the very thing we need most for life—air. We have also seen how our institutions have created social problems that often multiply the very ills that they intend to alleviate. Perhaps we are beginning to understand that the way we relate to others within our sphere, and especially those closest to us, determines not only our own comfort and pleasure but also has far-reaching and un-foreseeable effects on many lives.

One of life's greatest insecurities arises from the knowl-edge that we have the freedom to turn away from one another at any time. The closer we grow, the more intimately we are involved with another, the more we are aware of this possibil-ity. Each of us has different ways of handling this knowledge. One person may withdraw from close relationships; another may cling desperately to anyone who is kind. Some of us secretly hold back a part of ourselves from our relationships in order to avoid being devastated by loss. These coping mech-anisms may keep us emotionally safe, but ultimately it is a safety that harms us. Love is not a limited resource; the more we spend, the more there is to be spent. If we hold back our love, there will be less love available in the world.

A growing awareness of this principle in today's world has led to a quest on the part of many people to find new ways to experience and express love. Yet as long as our aware-ness of love as a personal reality is an intellectual one rather than one that arises from a deep sense of relatedness, our experiments in its name will only lead to yet another flight from true intimacy. Today's adult may be more sophisticated and less bound by rigid tradition in establishing relationships, but few of us are significantly more loving. It is easy to measure the extent of one's success in building truly creative and loving human relationships: it is reflected in the physical, emotional, mental, and spiritual well-being of those closest to us.

People may change, but love does not. Love can only become fuller or fade and disappear. In observing, reading about, or participating in the relationship experiments of the '60s and '70s, many of us have become accustomed to the idea of taking risks and trying out new ways of behaving with one another. While these experiments may not have brought more love into our lives, perhaps they have brought us to the point where we are willing to take some different kinds of risks, risks that will result in truly creative interpersonal relationships.

To do so, we need to learn more. Knowing that it is important to love is not enough; we need to learn what love really is and how to love well. We need to begin to distinguish truly loving behavior from the mere expenditure of emotion.

The oceanographic engineer observes the thrust and resistance of water and shore in order to understand the interaction of these powerful energies. These observations can be used to predict future configurations of the shoreline. What will be destroyed, and what might be created? Where will channels most likely open and close and what are the possible results of these changes? With a clear goal in mind, the engineer can determine how to use these energies to create new and different effects from those predicted. New systems can be introduced that will work with the flow of energy to achieve a creative result. Each mile of shoreline is unique. What works in Northern California, therefore, will be inappropriate in Southern Florida.

So it is with people. A mate, a child, a friend, each brings a special configuration of energy to interact with our own. Our energy also changes thrust and focus within the various types of relationships we have, just as the energy of others depends on how they perceive our relationship to them. Each relationship is unique, and at the same time, dependent on and connected to all of our other relationships. Finding the appropriate expression of love for friend, child, or mate involves an awareness of self, others, and our total constellation of relationships.

It is not easy to develop this kind of awareness. Our best tools for doing so lie in the arena of subjective experience. Feelings, intuitions, and informal observations are our most basic and potent collectors of information about our relationships. Yet we have learned to mistrust subjectivity without having a true perception of its strengths or limitations. Because of this mistrust, we have not developed our subjective talents as we have our intellectual strengths. We are out of contact with many of our feelings and have learned to ignore our intuition unless it can be substantiated with fact. If we are to be able to learn real love, it is necessary to resurrect the subjective, nonlogical side of our being and place it at an equal level with the rational, intellectual side. We need all the information we can get to handle life today. It will no longer serve us to glorify one side of our being at the expense of another. Only whole and harmoniously balanced people can truly love.

We may be on the verge of a revolution far greater than the Industrial Revolution or the onset of the Atomic Age. Because of the advances that have gone before, we are in a position, for the first time in history, to engage in a true human revolution, a revolution of the inner person that can encompass all ages, cultural backgrounds, and economic levels. We have the opportunity to choose to take the creative step to engage our energies with those of others in new and productive ways—ways that will build the inner structures that lead to an awareness of our real connection to all other people and, indeed, all other things in our world. Once we can do this, we will find that we no longer choose actions that harm those closest to us when we are trying to help and that the solutions we reach to ameliorate social problems do not create more devastating problems in their wake.

There is only one place to make a beginning. Our ability to join effectively with family, friends, peers, and society at large in creative ways is dependent upon our ability to accept and become one with self and those closest to us. Our best laboratory for understanding the world and our place in it is within our closest and most personal relationships. No matter how much we desire it, we cannot build a better world alone; nor can we build it out of lives that are flawed and full of conflict at the deepest, most personal level. We need to learn to love each other to create a world of love. And the place to start is wherever each one of us is at this moment.

2
Falling in Love Is Wonderful

One rare human experience is unforgettably unique and very special: the experience of falling in love. Most of us, if asked to share our memories of falling in love, would find the experience difficult to describe. We might remember that for a few hours, days, or weeks our world appeared transformed. The sun seemed to shine more brightly. We saw more beauty in a rainstorm, a flower, or the flight of a bird. Some would relate that the normal problems and irritations of daily life seemed less important. Most would recall feeling somehow more alive, more powerful and compassionate. Many remember an experience of apparently limitless energy, of breezing through the most tedious tasks with a smile. And it seemed that the whole world smiled back.

When love is new, our lover appears to be the ideal embodiment of all we desire in a companion. If our love is returned and we ourselves feel free to love, we embrace the experience with all the joy and enthusiasm of which we are capable.

In a very real way, the experience of falling in love is an experience of transcendence, of rising above our normal selves. We feel our usual protective barriers dissolving in the presence of the other. At times it seems as if our consciousness merges with our lover in perfect empathy and total harmony. We think each other's thoughts and feel one another's feelings. We communicate more with a look or a touch than we could with a lifetime of words. A love of the same book or a mutual passion for ice cream can symbolize the nearly mystical rightness and harmony we feel in one another's presence.

At its height the experience of transcendent love is a creative adventure. Whether or not we are moved to write poetry of our own, we can find new meaning in works of others. A fresh look may uncover great truth, even in passages we once thought absurdly sentimental. Daily events take on a new significance, and we may experience a feeling of connectedness with all things. We feel awed and possibly more than a little overwhelmed by the intensity of the experience and by the apparent newness of common events.

Somehow, inevitably, the passion passes. A misunderstanding, an insensitive remark, a small jealousy mars the perfect harmony we experienced together. We begin to see that our lover has flaws, has interests in things that bore us, has beliefs that we do not share, and qualities that we find unpleasant. Our sense of unity begins to slip away, the special sparkle fades from the world, and we sense ourselves to be ordinary people once more. Our love for one another may continue, but the experience of transcendence is lost.

Most of us respond to this change with a kind of wistful resignation. We speak of reaching a more mature and realistic stage in our relationship. Perhaps we are secretly a little relieved; so much consuming intensity has been frightening. Sometimes we may have wondered if we were losing ourselves in the other's personality. We may have feared that our thoughts and actions were not really our own and that we were beset by a kind of madness.

As time passes the memory of transcendent love grows pale. Ecstasy, like pain, is difficult to recreate. Occasionally a phrase, a place, or a snatch of a song will recall the experience in a haunting bittersweet fashion. We recognize the futility of reaching out to grasp the feeling. Most of us simply shrug and return to the task at hand, perhaps somewhat distracted for a time.

It is popular today to denigrate the experience we have when we fall in love. We call it immature romanticism, infatuation, or, if the lovers are very young, puppy love. We have learned to be somewhat cynical about love and view the behavior of lovers as flamboyant, excessive, or in slightly poor taste. We nod wisely to one another and feel a little superior in our knowledge that "it won't last."

Despite the transient nature of transcendent love, however, it is a completely valid and very important human experience. Transcendent love can teach us much about our capacity for joyous living. It is a demonstration of our potential for experiencing fulfillment in life. Transcendent love gives us an experience of what it feels like to function at our highest and most expanded levels of being. It gives us an opportunity to see how the world appears to us when we discard our fears and defensive boundaries and how we behave when we can operate without the limiting internal prohibitions that we usually carry with us into every situation.

The sensation of aliveness, enhanced perception and sensitivity, creativity, openness, and spontaneity that characterizes the transcendent love experience are similar to the qualities of self-actualized people described by Abraham Maslow in his classic investigation into the nature of optimum mental health. Falling in love gives us a preview of how we might experience all of life. It shows us where our continued growth as adults can take us. It is an experience of who we really are at the deepest and most profound levels of our humanness.

The central purpose of life is growth. All of us enter the world with the capacity for great joy and spontaneous aliveness. Our life task is to learn how to bring our innate capacities for joy and creativity into actuality through our daily activity. All of us feel more vital, more energetic, and closer to being fully alive at those times in life when we are learning a new skill, understanding a new concept, or finding out more about how to challenge what we believe to be our limits. To be growing is to be living life at its fullest.

Yet for many of us much of life is mostly routine. We go from day to day taking care of the necessary business of living without the sense of adventure and expanding possibilities that we feel during times of rapid growth. Sometimes we may wonder, like the girl in the song, if this is really all there is. Our brief experiences with transcendent love tells us there is more to life, but falling in love seems like a magic event that takes place out of time, outside our normal daily experience. We believe that the other is the source of our feeling. We convince ourselves that only the smile of good fortune can light up the world for us. That sense of aliveness, we believe, is out of our control and comes and goes by the whims of fate.

The very fact that this sense of vitality can burst out of us unexpectedly and at any time tells us that it is always a part of us, a part just waiting to be released. It is not fate or magic that opens us to these experiences, but our own beliefs that the environment is right and that it is safe to be who we really are. All of us can have more experiences of transcendence in our lives, but in order to do so, we first need to understand why we usually do not have them in the normal course of daily living. To find the answer we must go back to the experiences of early childhood.

A primary task for each child is to discover the ways that work to get attention, approval, and care from the adults in charge. Children are concerned about survival, for without survival there can be no growth. To the young child rejection may quite literally mean death. During the earliest years most children learn by trial and error what kinds of behavior will elicit a response from their parents.

As children, each of us needed to find effective ways to get attention and approval in our particular family. Some children learn that if they are cute and bubbly their parents pay more attention to them than if they are serious or solemn. If an older sibling is the cute and bubbly one, the child may decide that the way to get his or her share is to be shy and withdrawn. Another child may get approval by being the smart one, the funny one, or the creative one. Some find they get more attention by having tantrums, being clumsy, or getting sick. Children also learn what does not work well. In many families boys still learn that it is not appropriate to cry, and girls discover they must not act angry or get muddy if they want to be considered nice. As children practice their most effective attention and approval getting behaviors, these behaviors gradually become their habitual responses to most situations. These habitual responses form the basis for the roles that the individual will carry into later childhood and adulthood.

A child's tentative roles are tested and reinforced in play groups and schools and through interaction with grandparents and other adults. The result is that over time the child grows further and further from a spontaneous expression of real feelings and impulses. The roles we develop as a child can become so real to us over the years that it is possible to forget we were only playing a part and to begin to believe that the role is who we really are. We tend to label thoughts, impulses, and behavior that do not fit with our roles as bad or alien. As a result we all deny and disown important parts of ourselves as we are growing up. We become a little like the puppet Pinocchio—somewhere inside there is a real boy or girl, but that part of us is hard to find.

Our roles often serve us well in life. They are important in that they can help us get along with one another and reduce friction in daily living. They can help us get through difficult situations. For example, a writer friend of mine who hates large parties assumes her "author" role whenever she must attend a social affair. Instead of being uncomfortable and shy, she finds herself enthusiastically interviewing the other party-goers and usually has a wonderful time. Our roles can also help us make decisions and aid us in figuring out what to do with our lives. The comic on TV may have been the class clown. The person who learned to be helpful and kind to others to get approval as a child, may become involved in charitable activities as an adult.

As long as our roles promote our growth, help us to expand our talents, and to facilitate our relationships with others, we are comfortable with them. Sooner or later, however, we all come up against the limitations that are inherent in every role. Roles form a psychological blockade against those feelings and impulses that we have learned not to express for fear of rejection or disapproval from parents and other important people. As a role becomes more firmly established, we no longer have to consciously push away the feelings that are not consistent with it. It becomes an automatic process. These feelings do not go away, however. Feelings like anger and fear as well as aggressive and competitive impulses are a part of human experience. It requires an ongoing expenditure of large amounts of energy to keep them out of our conscious awareness. As a result a significant amount of the energy that we might use for growth is not available to us. It is tied up in maintaining a role.

In addition, since each role prohibits certain kinds of activity and experience, there may be many things we do not attempt because our roles will not allow it. Claudia has a lovely singing voice and often daydreams about performing before cheering crowds. Her idea of herself as wife and mother, however, does not include voice lessons and public appearances. Claudia cannot allow herself to take a step to develop a talent that could be a source of creative energy for her and of pleasure for others. She limits herself to bedtime lullabies for her children and occasionally sings in the shower. Our roles cease to serve us when they inhibit our growth. Life itself can begin to seem meaningless when we put the brakes on natural urges to learn more and expand our abilities.

The feelings that our roles prohibit can cause problems as well. Since these feelings stay with us, although usually outside of our awareness, they often find expression indirectly. The businessman who is under stress but cannot express his fear may develop ulcers or high blood pressure. The child who is angry at his mother may accidentally break a dish instead of becoming aware of his anger and risking rejection by expressing it. In addition, when we repress a part of our feelings, we close off the spontaneous experience of other feelings too. It's as if there is only one faucet for the feelings that make up our life energy to flow through. When we turn off some feelings, we reduce the flow to a trickle.

Falling in love is like turning on the faucet full blast. All at once we feel safe for a while to take down the role barriers and to experience and express all of the energy we have inside. We allow ourselves to experience our feelings much more strongly than ordinarily. We are more comfortable with them in all their intensity, because they are primarily positive, loving emotions. As we begin to express these feelings we learn that our new love will not reject us and is, in fact, enthusiastically receptive to hearing how we feel. Additionally, he or she supports us by sharing many of the same emotions. Lovers spend long hours just talking—opening up to one another and searching for new ways to express precisely how they feel. Creative energy flows synergistically and the experience builds until the lovers begin to see everything around them with fresh eyes and new understanding. The fears and inhibitions of the more familiar self are transcended by the formation of a partnership in which each participant feels totally understood and accepted as he or she really is beneath the façades present in normal interaction. The delight of sharing freely with another is enhanced by the experience of finding parts of the self that have been outside of awareness.

As roles drop away, life seems new and full of endless possibilities. We are growing, and it feels marvelous.

Fears and tensions build within the relationship as lovers grow increasingly intimate, and therefore, more vulnerable to one another. The more of the deeper self that is exposed, the greater the fear of possible rejection. As we begin to share things about ourselves perhaps never before revealed to another human, our apprehension increases. At some point each person reaches a degree of openness where old fears of rejection begin to outweigh the impulse to go forward. When one of the lovers begins to draw back, the other, sensing a change, may believe that the feared and half-expected rejection is occurring. This causes a reciprocal withdrawal, fears on both sides increase, and the upward spiral of transcendence ends. The relationship may terminate at this point, or it may move into a new phase in which partners begin to explore other aspects of relationship building.

If the relationship continues to grow after the stage of transcendent love has passed, disappointment at its loss is usually brief and is overshadowed by the new challenges the partners face. It is just as important for partners contemplating a long-term relationship to understand their differences as their similarities. After all, what we have heard about love usually has prepared us for the transience of transcendent love. We have had the once-in-a-lifetime experience; now we must move on.

If it were only the roles we play that prevent us from tapping the source of life energy within us, we would not find modifying them so difficult. Our roles are relatively easy to change. The mother who returns to school and the businessman who goes back to the land are changing their roles to find more room for growth. We all make adjustments, large or small, in our roles from time to time.

The problem is complicated by the fact that the beliefs we hold about the world operate to support us in continuing to play our roles. Roles are more or less difficult to change depending on the strength of the beliefs that support them. Each of us has a unique combination of assumptions and beliefs about life and our place in it. These comprise our point of view, the frame of reference through which we experience the events of life.

Frame of reference is based on conclusions we drew from experiences we have had in early childhood. An infant whose needs for food, warmth, and nurturing are met promptly and completely will experience a sense of security and probably conclude that the world is a safe place and that he or she is a worthwhile and lovable person. An infant who is frustrated in meeting important needs may conclude that people cannot be trusted.

Many different conclusions are possible. They are tentative deductions that do not come out of a rational process, but, rather emotional "decisions" that will be tested and retested through further experience. Nevertheless, they are very real aspects of the child's emerging world view and have a profound effect on the manner in which a child approaches his or her environment. As an adult, whether we greet new experiences with joyful anticipation or apprehension and fear, is largely determined by attitudes and beliefs first formed in early childhood. Since no one, no matter how loving the parents, has had a perfect childhood and has never been frustrated or misunderstood, we all have a frame of reference that contains some beliefs that help us and others that hinder us in later life.

Our frame of reference is like a magic pair of contact lenses through which we view the world. The lenses are constructed in such a way that we see some things very clearly and others in a distorted way. There are some things, too, that we do not see at all since each of us has blind spots and does not perceive those things that do not make sense within our frame of reference. Since we rarely (or never) remove these contact lenses and look at the world without our unique frame of reference, it seems to each of us that the way we see things is really the way they are. Each person's frame of reference has its own peculiar combination of clarity, distortion, and blind spots, so we all experience the world a little differently. Frame of reference is particularly evident when two people try to describe an argument or any intensely emotional experience they have shared. The descriptions sometimes differ so completely that it sounds as if they could not possibly be relating the same event.

It is in the nature of frame of reference that it appears true. Each of us experiences our frame of reference as so real and solid that it is hard to imagine that it is not the way things really are. We become so attached to certain aspects of it that we will defend it in the face of any opposition. Fathers have disinherited children and religious wars have been fought because of differences in frame of reference. But frame of reference is not purely a negative phenomenon; it is important to us because it helps us organize and understand our experience. It is through our frame of reference that we attribute the meaning to the situations that confront us in life that enables us to determine appropriate behavior and to solve problems. It is only when distortions and blind spots in our experience limit us or create more problems than they solve that frame of reference becomes troublesome, for without some basis of belief about the meaning of the events in our lives we would not be able to act at all.

Frame of reference, because of its appearance of truth, is very tenacious and difficult to change. We tend to condition and recondition our frame of reference through a mechanism called selective perception. None of us can attend to all the stimuli in our environment at any given moment. We would be overwhelmed if we were forced to process all the sounds, sensations, thoughts, feelings, and happenings that are available for us in any moment. In each situation we concentrate on those aspects that have meaning for us at that time. When we drive down a highway at high speed in heavy traffic, we usually do not see the roadside flowers, the distant mountains, or the beauty in the cloud formations. We may not really be aware of the music on the car radio, yet will instantly hear a distant siren or the squeal of brakes from the next car. During the first U.S. manned space flight, drivers pulled over to the side of the road to listen to the countdown and liftoff because they could not drive safely while concentrating on the radio report.

Chuck and George do business regularly, and neither looks forward to their frequent meetings. Chuck's frame of reference contains a belief that people are untrustworthy. He is suspicious of George and invests a great deal of energy in attending to cues that will help him decide whether or not to trust George to uphold his part of their current contract. George, on the other hand, believes that his worth is dependent upon his ability to please other people. He listens carefully to Chuck to find out what Chuck wants to hear and then tries to say those things. Chuck senses George's wishy-washy position and George picks up on Chuck's suspicion and disapproval. Their business dealings are unpleasant for both of them and act to reinforce their individual frames of reference. Sensing George's insecurity, Chuck can tell himself that here is yet another example of untrustworthiness. George, having failed to please, has more evidence of what he believes to be his basic worthlessness. Frame of reference operates like a self-fulfilling prophecy. We act on the basis of our beliefs, creating outcomes that conform to our belief systems.

When we fall in love our frame of reference expands. People in love find new and different meanings in common situations. In fact, the experience we call insight is simply a sudden expansion of frame of reference. New insights come rapidly in transcendent love. A person who has been wary of others learns that it is possible to trust and share openly. A person who feels worthless can learn that another will value him if he feels valuable himself. These insights can generalize from our experience of the loved one to other areas in our lives. Transcendent love gives us the opportunity to transform all our relationships, to see the world as loving and supportive, to feel at home with life.

The transcendent love experience does not really depend on anything outside of us. It is something we feel when we drop our roles and begin to expand our frame of reference. When the frame of reference stops expanding, we pick up our roles and retreat from the experience. We reinforce our beliefs that we are dependent upon a certain type of response from the other to continue expanding because the experience ends as we close down the free flow of our own feelings. The reality is that transcendence depends only on our own willingness to continue to expand our frames of reference to encompass and understand the differences we experience in one another as well as the similarities. Transcendent love is both a creator and a by-product of growth, and we each have within us the power to bring more of this kind of love into our lives.

3

Traditional Marriage Versus Alternative Relationships

According to our traditional beliefs about love and marriage, falling in love is a once-in-a-lifetime experience. The romantic myth of song and story tells us that one day we will meet and fall hopelessly in love with our perfect mate. Just as day follows night, we will then marry and live happily ever after.

Deviation from this pattern is the stuff of tragedy. We cannot imagine Romeo or Juliet living on to love another with even half the passion. Lovers who do marry and find themselves unable to sustain a fulfilling relationship with one another may be seen as sick, immoral, or immature. We may view the loss of love as a personal failing to be kept secret from the world and, as much as possible, from ourselves, or we may rationalize that we have moved into a more "mature" phase of our relationship.

Fortunately, the myth is wrong. People can and do fall in love more than once and in the same deeply fulfilling ways. Should a relationship fail, people will often find another love as powerful as the first. Living happily ever after, however, often presents more of a problem. In fact, it almost seems as if marriage and family life as we know it today is designed to kill transcendent love forever. How is it possible to rise above normal experience when the majority of contact between partners revolves around keeping up with the bills, making sure the kids eat right, and resting up to go at it another day? Coping with the stress of daily living can consume so much energy that we are often grateful if our relationship is good enough to allow us to feel like holding one another for a moment before sleep and to enjoy an occasional evening out together.

Although modern marriage and family life are quite different from the marriages of even 200 years ago, a look at the historical antecedents of today's marriages in the light of our evolving relationship needs can help illuminate some of the problems we experience. Marriage as an institution is based on ancient biological and economic necessity. Rather than going together like a horse and carriage, love and marriage, while not necessarily mutually exclusive, have been irrelevant to one another until very recently. Marriage was designed to provide for the care of the products of sexual passion and to form a team to enhance the economic stability and increase the likelihood of physical survival of its members. Religious and civil law elaborated the rules of marriage which, while they differed at different times and in different cultures, all served to preserve social order by defining the rights and obligations of the partners and their respective family members. Neither love nor human compassion nor a sense of individual responsibility have ever been enough to insure cooperation when economic factors are at issue. Thus, while there has been a good deal of emphasis on the spiritual aspects of the marriage contract in many cultures, the prevailing religious rules tended to support the economic structure. In some cultures there have been formal or *de facto* differences in marriage customs for the lower and upper classes because of the aristocracy's greater concerns with the economic and political ramifications of their unions. Often there was provision, in custom if not law, for the expression of love outside of marriage, particularly for the upper classes. During the Age of Chivalry elaborate rules for conducting supposedly nonsexual extramarital romantic relationships were developed by ladies of the aristocracy. In ancient Greece the idealized love was between men rather than man and woman, thus eliminating any possible confusion about the purpose of marital relationships.

As our economic wealth increases and technological and social advances make us less dependent on one another for survival, our uncertainty about the purpose of marriage increases. It is no longer a necessity to marry solely for economic protection or even for social approval. Today a "marriage of convenience" is even somewhat dishonorable, something to pity if not to scorn. Currently we believe that we marry for love. On the other hand we tend to remain married for sexual convenience, for the sake of the children, to maintain our standard of living ("We can't afford a divorce") and because we have arrived at an advantageous division of labor to support our daily existence ("I make the money; she pays the bills and takes care of the house"). With all the economic and social burdens that today's marriage continues to carry, the nurturing of real love quickly slips to a low position on the list of priorities. We *want* to marry for love. We want our intimacy to deepen and our emotions to expand in the sharing of our mutual life tasks. But for this to happen we must take risks in communication and action that may threaten the stability of the union. Partners often choose not to discuss business problems, attractions to other people, boredom in the relationship, or interpersonal conflicts in order to keep the peace. The more our inner feelings and concerns are not shared, regardless of the reasons, the more we lose contact with real people inside and develop roles that we hope will preserve the relationship. It is impossible to maintain an intimate and loving relationship with a role. A person playing a role may be an effective and competent financial partner, a responsible parent, a charming companion, and even a competent and inventive sexual partner, but not an intimate. There is nothing at the center of a role to love from and nothing to contact there for the expression of real love. A role is form without essence, an elaborate mirage.

While the traditional functions of institutionalized marriage create confusion about what we are doing with one another, and how we are to do it, our language further obscures the situation. We all want to love and be loved, but when we say this what do we mean? We are aware of differences in the meanings of the feelings we are expressing when we say we love our mother, our child, our pet, and our neighbor's new curtains. But because our language does not support us in making distinctions among nuances of positive feeling, we find it difficult to think clearly about the subjective differences in our experience. When we say we need love or want to love we are really using a rather vague, catch-all term that can have an infinite number of meanings depending on the situation and our state of mind at the moment. For example, we may mean that we need a hug or loving touch right then. We may mean we are lonely and want to be assured of long-term companionship. We may mean we want a child to care for or a new fur coat or some peace and quiet to complete an important project. Think of the times you have said or thought "If he/she really loved me . . ." and you will begin to develop an idea of how many unrelated and often contradictory definitions we all have of love.

Since our concept of love encompasses so many different experiences, needs, and behaviors, it is hard for any of us to argue that we do not have love in our lives. Nearly everyone has someone who says they love them—mother, child, friend, or mate. As we look at our relationships and see that many of them can be defined as loving ones, we can add to our confusion about love by concluding that any dissatisfaction we experience is either the result of a personal flaw or has to do with some other problem unrelated to love.

Our historical traditions, religious and moral values, socially approved roles and lifestyles, and the imprecision of our language all contribute to an increasing personal confusion that is resulting in a major crisis in relationships today. More and more adults are experiencing a growing sense of how ill-suited their closest relationships seem to be in meeting their deepest emotional needs. Scratch the surface of today's family man or woman and you are likely to find not the deep contentment and sense of fulfillment we would hope to see, but an uneasy sense of being a square peg in a round hole. We do not seem to fit somehow, but we become strangely inarticulate when asked to explain. The truth is that there is growing dissatisfaction with the quality of our mutual interaction, but we cannot pinpoint the source of our problem and therefore have no idea what to do about it. We feel not only confused, but helpless, and, in our impotence, tend to turn on one another, the institution of marriage, and the structure of society itself as the culprits.

Certainly we can find plenty to fault in all of these areas. At the personal level conflicts over finances, sex, child rearing, leisure time, housekeeping standards (the list is endless) can serve both to keep us involved with one another and to obscure the real problems that underlie a sense of lack of fulfillment and alienation from one another. Sociologists and philosophers have been telling us for several generations that our social institutions are more harmful than helpful in promoting material and emotional well-being. Our schools promote mediocrity rather than creativity. Our economy supports uneven distribution of resources and exploitation of the many by the few. Our political system is unresponsive to the needs of the individual and only minimally effective in mediating among individual needs to achieve the common good. Technological proliferation creates more problems than it solves, alienates us from our environment, and threatens our very lives by polluting our air and poisoning our food. Marriage and family, formerly viewed at least in principle as a source of stability and solace within a stressful and often antihuman environment, is now under attack for limiting personal freedom and perpetuating neurotic patterns. Rather than being seen as supportive and nurturing, marriage is increasingly being viewed as more or less crippling to husbands, wives, and the children of their union. Thus marriage is now seen by many as a trade-off. We sacrifice certain opportunities for growth and adventure for security and social acceptability, and the value of making this trade-off is being vigorously questioned.

In recent decades our dissatisfaction has grown as the quality of life on the material level has improved. We have learned that labor-saving devices, homeownership, salary raises, and increased leisure time have not created the happiness that we once expected. The more we find that this or that new toy is not going to bring us the happiness we seek, the more we secretly despair. Alcoholism, abuse of prescription drugs, and divorce increase at a faster rate among those most privileged materially.

A rather striking symptom of our dissatisfaction is the recent trend toward relationship experiments. As it becomes clearer that success, power, and wealth are not going to give us the satisfactions we seek, we have turned to our personal relationships. In recent years we have seen experiments in communal living, group marriage, and contractural marriage. Many have rejected marriage for monogamous or nonmonogamous live-in or partial live-in situations. Others have tried out various more or less formalized sexual trading, ranging from open marriage to swinging to the more traditional clandestine affair. Serial monogamy is seen by some as the ideal for adults today. At the other end of the spectrum, proponents of free love continue to claim to have the solution to all our problems.

These experiments have proved to be both admirable and tragic. While some couples have undertaken new relationship forms out of a lack of commitment to the primary relationship or in irresponsible naiveté, many experimenters made this choice from a realization both of the importance of their primary bond and a desire to meet strong needs without burdening their relationship unrealistically. Experimenters believed they would have more to offer and be less likely to take out personal frustrations on the relationship under these circumstances. Many hoped for more emotional equality within the primary relationship or that a spark of freshness and adventure would enhance relationships that had fallen into routine and deadening patterns.

The alternative form chosen by each couple depended on what important personal needs and desires they felt could not be fulfilled with one another. If the lack was a sexual one, partners were likely to choose swinging, wife swapping, or similar methods for establishing nonemotional sexual liaisons. If more emotional and deep friendship needs were involved, some form of open marriage or intimate friendship was often chosen. A desire for a richer family life led partners to seek a group marriage or a communal living situation, with or without sexual sharing.

Each experiment has its own specific rules or mutually agreed norms. There have probably been nearly as many variations in rules as experiments. How much information is to be shared; when, under what circumstances, and with whom sexual contact is allowed, and what the responsibilities of primary partners are to one another has been determined by the needs and fears of the couple. Rules are meant to protect the primary relationship from threat and conflict and to support the goal of enhancing the couple's bond.

It takes courage to break out of traditional forms and to attempt in good faith to evolve new forms of relating that will incorporate deeper human values. We can admire the courage of those who have risked their most precious relationships hoping to find more fulfilling ways of loving one another. Those who have been willing to take these risks have done a service to all of us. They have articulated questions that are central to the survival of loving relationships in today's world and they have allowed us the opportunity to discover how well certain solutions to the problems of boredom, alienation, and loss of passion will work.

Research on long-term outcomes of relationship experiments is scanty. In most of the research that has been done the emotional position of the researcher has had an impact on the conclusions drawn. Additionally, relationship experimenters themselves often have strong ideological convictions and naturally want very badly for their alternatives to turn out positively. Sex and sexual sharing particularly are highly charged emotional issues that very few people can approach dispassionately however hard they try. Much of the experimentation has gone underground in recent years after a great deal of public attention was focused on alternative relationships in the early 1970s. Many questions have not been answered, and the jury is still out on the question of whether nonmonogamous intimate relationships is neurotic acting out or a healthy adaption to the realities of contemporary life.

We do, however, know something about the outcomes of some of these experiments. Just as the early stages of a political revolution brings chaos to the social system, so have many experiments in alternative relationships resulted in confusion and pain for the participants. For example, one group of fifteen families began exploring alternative relationships in 1972. They had strong friendship bonds established over many years association. As a group they read extensively and discussed the alternatives with one another for some time before actually embarking on an experiment. Each couple worked out its own rules, and a variety of different arrangements were tried. By 1978 none of the original couples remained married to one another, nor had any of the liaisons formed with other group members endured. Only a few of the thirty adults involved were willing to discuss their experience and all of them were both saddened and shaken by the intensity of the pain they had felt and seen their friends experience. They expressed concern for their children. Almost without exception they felt great reluctance to engage in any deeply intimate commitment in the foreseeable future. Yet most of them would not conclude that alternative relationships could not work out happily. They only felt that they themselves had not been able to find the way to do this. Many were still strongly favorable to alternative relationships in theory, on the grounds that traditional marriage relationships are not enhancing to human growth.

When a scientist looking for a new substance accidently blows up the laboratory, he or she will carefully examine what has been learned from the process and try another method, possibly with improved forethought and planning. We, too, can learn a great deal from the experience of relationship experimenters. At the least, we can see how strongly our security needs demand to be taken into account. Multiple sexual or love relationships appear to cause more problems than they solve. We may now be able to acknowledge our security needs more freely without feeling compelled to label them childish or neurotic. We have also learned some important truths about love itself and the extent to which the ability to experience more love has become crucial to many individuals today. Now that our dissatisfactions with love have been more clearly articulated, we may be able to take the next step to transcend what previously seemed to be an irreconcilable conflict between the needs for stability and for passionate excitement in intimate partnerships.

4

Combining the Best of Both Worlds: A New Look at Love and Commitment

When the Class of '59 graduated from high school the young men and women embarking on adult life had a firm idea of the choices they needed to make to move into the next stage of their development. The men knew they had three responsible alternatives: going to college or technical school, signing up for military service, or finding a job immediately. Sooner or later they would all have to make a commitment to some kind of job or career, get married, and raise a family. The women's choices were even clearer. Their destiny was to marry, have children, and become full-time homemakers. The only question was where and how to find the right man. Some were already displaying tiny diamonds on the third finger left hand. Others planned to work or go to college in the hiatus between high school and marriage. A few also spoke bravely of a career, usually teaching or nursing—good careers to fall back on or to pick up again after the child-rearing years. To many these choices may not have seemed particularly exciting, but there was no doubt that they were the ones that would open the door to responsible and successful adulthood.

Just twenty years later the situation was drastically different. The Class of '79 was confronted with a multiplicity of alternatives and no guarantee that choosing any one over another would lead to success, respect, or satisfaction. Only one thing remained clear; somehow one must arrange for a source of food and shelter. Beyond that the options seemed endless and the advice of peers, parents, and counselors more confusing than helpful.

The social changes occurring in that twenty-year interval created a situation that virtually eliminated the possibility of making any important life decision primarily out of a desire for social approval or a wish to be guided by the wisdom of those who had gone before. For example, nearly every career choice available to the Class of '79 was disapproved by a significant segment of the population. Business success was seen by some as materialistic and exploitive. Working with one's hands could be seen as either dehumanizing or irresponsible, depending on the work setting. Social servants were viewed by many as leeches on society, power-mad manipulators, or unrealistic dreamers. The value of work itself was in question. For every proponent of a particular point of view, three or four detractors with arguments equally strong and apparently just as valid could be found. It has become increasingly clear to all of us that we cannot expect society to provide us with the absolute standards for evaluating the correctness or appropriateness of very many of the important life decisions we must make. In fact, a look at society today raises far more questions than we will probably be able to answer in our lifetime.

This situation is particularly upsetting in our personal relationships. We still have the same old needs and desires: we want love, security, intimacy, sexual satisfaction, a sense of continuity and stability, a level of excitement and passion. But it seems that no one can tell us how to put together relationships that will enable us to get what we want. In fact, it often appears that we want the impossible. If we look at marriage or any similar long-term commitment from one perspective it seems to offer the advantages of stability and security and the opportunity to form a trusting mutually nurturing partnership with another that can deepen and grow over a lifetime. Marriage promises the joys of warmth and sharing from day to day, of creating something enduring and valuable with another, of growing in the mutual give and take of family life. From another perspective, however, marriage can seem a trap, an impossible burden, an overwhelming responsibility. We can envision year after year lessening spontaneity and increasing boredom and frustration. Marriage can limit our freedom to experience new things, to grow, and to express ourselves in new and creative ways. It threatens to lead to a dull, deadening routine of meeting the needs, demands, and expectations of others at the expense of our own growth and personal satisfaction. It replaces love with guilt and intimacy with the contempt of familiarity.

When we look at alternatives to traditional monogamous marriage we are thrust into the same kind of dilemma. Single people are free to experiment and find adventure. They can make choices about how to spend an evening or a lifetime without needing to consider the priorities or expectations of anyone else. They must answer to no one but their own wishes and desires. But this has its drawbacks too. Single people can be lonely. Singlehood raises questions about the ultimate meaning of a life with no strong connections to others. Single people may miss loving companionship or grow weary of the ups and downs of relationships that do not develop beyond a relatively superficial level. As we saw in Chapter Three, attempts to combine the excitement and adventure of new kinds of intimate relationships with marriage or other forms of primary commitments have had their own disadvantages and problems. No where, it seems, is there a structure that supports the kind of relationships we crave. In every case, it looks as if we must sacrifice some important needs to meet others equally important.

This situation is an example of what psychologists call the classic double bind and others more straightforwardly refer to as "damned if you do and damned if you don't." For couples who sincerely desire the intensity of their feelings for one another to last, for their involvement with each other to deepen, and to bring joy rather than pain into their life together, the dilemma is particularly distressing. Many people have reached a point where the fear of commitment is so equally balanced with the deep wish to love and be loved that they are frozen in indecision. The stress generated by this kind of existential conflict, both on relationships and within the individual, may ultimately become as painful or as deadening as going forward or retreating would have been.

To resolve this dilemma we need to begin to broaden our frame of reference about love and relationships. Instead of looking without for new structures and forms for relationships, we can begin to look inward at the attitudes and assumptions we carry into our relationships. This inward exploration is not meant as a search for our lacks or weaknesses but as a way to identify the strengths and capacities for relating that we have forgotten or never seen.

Part of our problem comes from the psychological perspectives that permeate society. Traditional psychology has been built on an incomplete and somewhat flawed view of the nature of humankind. Freud, whose ground-breaking work on the nature of the unconscious mind has opened many doors to a fuller understanding of human nature, believed that the newborn child enters the world a small bundle of aggressive and destructive impulses. In order to become capable of living in society, the child must become civilized. From this viewpoint, effective parenting is seen as the process of training the natural antisocial tendencies out of the child and providing a strong super-ego, or conscience, which would act to restrain the chaotic, animalistic desires of the id. Antisocial behavior in children and adults is therefore "natural" and is the result of incomplete training. Positive training results in the re-directing of these impulses into socially acceptable channels of expression.

Neurosis is a conflict between super-ego and id that results in inappropriate and nonproductive channeling of impulses. These ideas have been widely accepted, particularly in Christian cultures, because of their compatability with the popular version of the notion of original sin. The attitudes growing out of beliefs about the essential evil of human nature permeate all levels of society and determine how we approach most social and personal problems. The effect on human relationships is staggering. We expect the worst of ourselves and one another. We become suspicious of everyone's motives, including our own. We find moral issues confusing and being and doing "good" often nearly impossible. We grow cynical about the possibilities of having good relationships or of leading the good life.

In recent years humanistic and transpersonal psychology have put forth a substantially different view of human nature. Humanistic psychology asserts that we are born with both creative and destructive capacities and that it is the nature of the child's early experiences that determine whether or not his or her ultimate behavior will be socially and personally positive or negative. Specifically, the personality will reflect how well the universal basic needs for warmth, food, shelter, and nurturing have been met in early childhood. If these needs have been met fully, the growing child and adult will be able to meet higher level needs for sexual expression, love, and respect and perhaps ultimately reach a full expression of the inherent qualities of truth, beauty, and goodness that are the goal of human development. Destructive, antisocial, or neurotic behaviors are seen as expressions of deficiencies in basic need fulfillment and ways that the personality have developed to deal with a frustration or inability to meet one or more of the basic needs.

Transpersonal psychology takes this new view of humankind a step further. This emerging branch of psychology asserts that at the most basic and purest levels of our being we are, at birth and all through life, a living and material expression of the qualities of love, joy, creativity, power, knowledge, and unity that characterize the infinite. The underlying purpose of life is to grow in such a way that we expand our ability to express these qualities in concrete, practical ways within the material world. Our experiences, beginning in the womb and continuing from birth all through life, either aid or inhibit our ability to learn the skills that will enable us to expand our ability to express our basic nature. Since the expectations of society and parents do not include an awareness of this reality, early experiences generally do not support and, in fact, are often counterproductive to the development of these qualities. As a result, and in order to get along in a world that is based on a totally different vision of reality, the child hides and ultimately forgets his or her essence and develops the roles and behaviors necessary to ensure survival. Conflict, pain, and negative behavior are the natural results of alienation from the deepest and most fundamental aspects of the personality. Failure to expand and express those fundamental qualities leads to anxiety, suffering, and a sense of personal insecurity that we try to overcome by playing our approved roles more and better. This is an effort that is ultimately doomed to failure, since real satisfaction in life can only be found by resurrecting the essential self and learning to translate its qualities effectively in our activity within the real world. The subconscious is seen not as Freud's seething cauldron of destructive, animalistic urges, but as the source and symbolic expression of our forgotten true nature. Feelings, dreams, fantasies, and random mental images that arise spontaneously are the statements from our subconscious about the relationship between our conscious ego and our unconscious essential self.

The essential self, then, is that part of each one of us that is most basic and real. It is what remains when we drop our roles, beliefs, transient emotional expressions, personality characteristics, and personal quirks. It is that "you" that has always been with you, unchanged from earliest memory. It has been variously named the real self, the true self, the soul, the I AM. It is more, however, than a psychological concept or philosophical theory; it is the essence that each of us holds and the essential fount of vital energy that supports our physical, mental, and emotional lives. Everyone has an experience of the essential self. It is difficult for us to isolate and examine this experience because the essential self is the experiencer within each one of us. Trying to investigate it directly is like trying to see your eyes.

The nonlogical and emotional aspects of life provide a mirror for a partial viewing of the essential self. Music, art, dance, intuition, and love are a few vehicles that can put us in touch with this lost part of ourselves. Peak experiences, creative inspiration, and the euphoria reported by some runners and a few other athletes, are all partial experiences of what lies at our inner core. Meditation techniques that relax the body and quiet the mind can provide an experience of the self that remains beyond thought, feeling, mental image, and physical sensation. Some people have used hallucinogenic drugs, fasting, or sensory deprivation to learn more about the self that endures when normal patterns of mental and physical absorbtion are interrupted. Simply quietly and lovingly being in the presence of a very young child can teach us much about the true essence of humankind.

Perhaps the most common experience of the essential self is the one we have when we fall in love. The joy, the creativity, the sense of power, the boundless energy, and the deep intuitive knowing of another that are part of the transcendent love experience are qualities of the essential self manifesting in life. To understand love, we need to understand that it has little to do with the object of our love. Love is an experience of our own deepest reality. Its dependency on anything outside ourself is illusionary. In fact, the relationship of the experience of love to the loved one is quite different from what we normally assume it to be.

When we fall in love it appears that it is the special qualities, the pleasing personality, the physical attractiveness, or the inner beauty of the loved one that causes us to experience the happiness and joy that we feel in his or her presence. Their liveliness, their beauty, their warmth, seem to warm and enliven us. It seems as if our lover is like a campfire. We are attracted to the circle of warmth that the lover radiates and feel beautiful and brightened by the reflection of his or her glory.

In fact, the object of our love is more like a mirror. The qualities that attract us are qualities we have within but may not have perceived clearly or been able to express satisfactorily. We are drawn to another because we want to experience ourselves as expressing more fully the qualities that we perceive in that person. The greatest joy of being in love does not lie in the fact that someone whom we see as very special and valuable also values us, but in the opportunity we ourselves have to experience and acknowledge some of our own inner values that we had previously not recognized. Falling in love with another is, in a way, really falling in love with oneself.

Very often people are surprised when they learn that someone they love returns the feeling. We hope (and yet fear to hope) that it will be so, and when we find that it is, we may believe we are experiencing incredibly good fortune. Yet it is the nature of love that more than likely people who attract us will also be attracted to us if they are open to looking at us at all. If the qualities we see and like in another are actually a mirror of our own qualities, then obviously we are also a mirror for the other. They, too, will have an opportunity to see in us the things in themselves that are most basic and essential to their own experience of their deepest nature.

The really amazing thing about love is that we do not

fall in love more often. It is potentially possible to fall in love with everyone we meet. The essential self, the true nature of every human person is the same. We are all creative, loving, beautiful, harmonious, powerful, compassionate, playful, joyous spirits who have allowed those capacities to become thwarted, hidden, re-directed, or submerged to a greater or lesser extent depending on the experiences we have had and the decisions we made about ourselves, others, and the nature of the world. In this sense we are all potentially mirrors for one another. Whom we fall in love with depends on our own beliefs about love and who is appropriate to love, which qualities we need most to express at any point in our development, the roles we enjoy playing and the activities we enjoy engaging in, our openness to loving, the personality of the other, the kinds of relationships we consciously or unconsciously know we need to develop in order to grow, and often on factors as insignificant as chance and propinquity.

Loving one another is normal. What is abnormal is that it is not our usual experience. One of the deepest truths about life is that it requires the expenditure of a great deal of energy not to care. To avoid loving one another we must hold on to the fear of knowing ourselves or another at a deep level. We must defend ourselves against allowing others to come close enough to really see us. We must maintain barriers of mistrust, hostility, and even hatred. We must pretend to ourselves and one another that we do not need, desire, or value sharing and intimacy. We must devalue the intuitive knowledge that the symbols of success, achievement, and material comfort we strive for do not fulfill our deepest needs. To avoid loving we must stay in constant conflict with our essential selves and develop increasingly complex and even more distracting methods to handle the resulting anxiety and despair.

The way out of this dilemma involves beginning to look at love and intimate relationships in some new ways. By itself, the fact that we experience love in the presence of another is not a particularly good reason to make a commitment to a relationship with that person. For two people to marry or decide to build a life together simply and only because they are in love, is bound to lead to personal confusion and disillusionment with the relationship. When the experience of love changes and the times when they do not feel loving inevitably arrive, the relationship will be threatened. At these times partners will either move to terminate their connection or feel trapped within the mutual economic and social forms they have established together. Each will blame the other for the loss of love, because they believe the other was responsible for the presence of it. Similarly, they will see the other as the source of their current misery or dissatisfaction. As long as we continue to believe that our feelings are caused by something outside of us and that our ability to experience satisfaction depends solely or primarily on our partner's behavior and attitudes, then we will continue to miss every opportunity to experience the real and abundant value of making a lasting commitment to sharing life with another human being.

The true value of relationships lies in their power to demonstrate for us all the ways in which we resist love and hide our true selves from one another. Relationships provide a potent illustration of the contrast between how we feel when we act from the center of our being and what life is like for us when we withdraw from that experience. Very simply, an intimate relationship works and feels marvelous when we allow ourselves to be real with one another and it gets stuck and feels miserable when we do not. A relationship that is based on a mutual commitment to learning how to be real with one another under all circumstances will never be threatened. We will always know what we are doing together at any given time; either we are growing in our ability to be real or we are exhibiting and experiencing our individual barriers to authenticity. Either way, we are being true to our purpose and commitment to one another. When we understand our relationship this way, it is impossible to betray one another. No matter what our feelings or behavior happens to be at any moment, we will be opening up opportunities for self and partner to learn important truths about life and love. We will be able to see our economic interdependence, our mutual responsibility to children, our social status, and routines of daily life together as forms that support learning and growth rather than primary sources of satisfaction or irritating realities that chain us together.

If we can begin to look at intimate relationships from this perspective, many exciting possibilities open up. We can learn that there is no real conflict between individual freedom and responsibility to one another. In fact, they are both aspects of a fundamental human condition. The feelings we sometimes have of being torn between meeting our own needs or meeting the needs of others only mean that we are not looking at the situation from a broad enough perspective. The fundamental issue is how we can become everything that we intuitively know we can be. At those times when we are living up to our potential, we will always feel satisfied. The circumstances that arise in our lives are nothing but opportunities for us to exercise our capacities. If we feel burdened by what we perceive to be the demands of others, then we have not yet seen the opportunity they are offering us to grow and become more of who we really want to be. Sometimes they are showing us that we have become one-sided or unbalanced in the qualities that we have chosen to develop. At other times it could be that we have made people unnecessarily dependent on us and we need to learn to support them in learning their own strengths instead of taking care of them. It is not unusual for people to find they have set their lives up in such a way as to inhibit growth rather than promote it. When we do this, our lives will be full of people and events that seem to be forcefully pointing this out to us.

Often it is only through hindsight that we understand the meaning of certain situations that we have faced. The interesting thing about life is that it is invariably bringing us exactly the situations that we need to confront in order to wake up to the fact that we alone are the source of our satisfaction. The exercise of freedom is only satisfying to us when the choices we make support our personal evolution. Since we cannot evolve in any other way than through effective activity in the world, our responsibility to ourselves and to the world around us are really always complimentary. Any conflict we perceive is an illusion that we need to remove in order to become truly free.

This view of relationships also allows us to see the real possibilities for achieving our heart's desire with one another: the excitement of an on-going passionate connection within the security of a stable relationship that endures through the embracing of problems rather than resistance to them. We really cannot lose our love for one another; we can only hide from it. Breaking off relationships is difficult and painful because at some deep level we know that beyond all the anger and sorrow we may have experienced together, our love still lurks in the shadows. Many couples find that their positive feelings for one another re-emerge at the point where a break is definite and irreversible. Although this does not seem to make sense within our usual belief system about love, it looks perfectly reasonable when we recognize the reality that love is the natural experience we have together and that it has nothing to do with whether or not we are capable of having a good relationship together.

Good relationships are built on willingness to take responsibility for feeling and exhibiting love for one another, and on the extent to which our individual purposes and intentions in the relationship and in life compliment and support each other. To have a good relationship it is important to choose someone whose style of reacting and personality are compatible enough with our own to make it easy for us to be together. A relationship that is both secure and passionate can be formed when both partners are clear that everything that happens between them, whether it brings pleasure or pain, is only another opportunity to learn more about themselves and the meaning of their own life. If we can take advantage of these opportunities, learning the lessons they offer, we will have a chance to fall in love with one another again and again. Each time partners can work together to expand their ability to experience and express more of their essential selves with one another, new passion will be released into their relationship.

The security in such a relationship arises from the fact that our basic expectations are always being met. We know and take responsibility for the knowledge that we are always providing a mirror for one another and inviting each other to grow. Whatever our problems and pleasures are with one another, we have the opportunity to learn something about our essential selves, and we recognize that our experience of satisfaction or discomfort depends entirely on our ability at that moment to expand and become proficient in communicating and exercising the qualities we are developing. When we perceive the other as a barrier, we have an opportunity both to share information he or she may need and at the same time to realize that a barrier is the "exercycle" of life that will enable us to gain the strength we require to meet the next challenge down the road.

We never "get there" in life. The only place we will arrive at is our own death. Life is nothing more than a constant parade of challenges. Our freedom is the freedom to respond to or reject the challenges. Happiness is in deciding to feel good about choosing to respond and in having the skills to meet the challenges effectively. The intense personal conflicts that intimate relationships illuminate provide an unparalleled avenue for learning how to do this.

5

Happily Ever After and Other Relationship Myths

Growing up means growing aware of the promises of adult love. Many classic children's stories are glittering romances, and little girls still like to imagine themselves transformed by love's first kiss. Little boys see themselves as knights in shining armor performing great feats to save distressed damsels. The rock star or truck-driving heroes of modern cinema are just up-to-date incarnations of Prince Charming. As the hero wins the love of his liberated career-girl princess in the final fade-out, we know we are to add "and they lived happily ever after" to the credits appearing on the screen.

No matter how cynical and sophisticated we become about love, there is still a small piece of each of us that vibrates in response to the idea of living happily ever after. The ways of love, after all, are mysterious and unfathomable. Perhaps there really is a magic golden kingdom where anger and dissatisfaction have been banished forever. Perhaps there is one culture where the child-rearing practices or family structure prevent jealousy and boredom from occurring between husband and wives. Perhaps it is true that there is one perfect soul mate for each of us and that if we could find that person, we would live forever in a state of limitless bliss.

The myths of childhood live on, teasing and tantalizing us as adults. They are evident in the questions we sometimes ask ourselves about love: What is true love? How will I know when it's the real thing? What if it's only chemistry between us? These myths are apparent, too, in that vague uneasiness, that sense of never being totally sure we are making the right choices in love. What is the truth in our myths about love and where are these myths leading us astray? How do our beliefs about love prevent us from being effective in real-life relationships?

Myth Number One: The Myth of the Perfect Partner. The story of Cinderella beautifully illustrates one of our oldest and most dear love myths. Somewhere in the world lives our other half, the perfect soul mate whose destiny is inextricably intertwined with our own. It is our task to seek out this person and, although the odds are heavily against our ever finding one another, if we pursue the quest with integrity and a true heart, the way will open up for us. We will know our true love by a sign. Bells will ring, the glass slipper will fit. Perhaps we will both love the same music, poetry, or ice cream. Once we find each other we must never let each other go. Though the quest may be arduous, we are guaranteed never-ending love if our character is strong enough to overcome whatever barriers lie in our path.

Most of us are well aware that we have never developed the purity of heart necessary to qualify as a Prince Charming or Cinderella. However, it is in the nature of love that many of us will meet someone who initially appears to be the perfect soul mate. When we discover that we are not going to live happily ever after, we can become confused and upset over the difference between our perhaps only half admitted hopes and reality. If the relationship does not last we may wonder if we have missed our once-in-a-lifetime chance for love through some personal failing. Should the relationship endure, the differences between us may cause us to conclude that we have made an error in judgment. This was not the true soul mate we sought, but only an approximation—a cleverly packaged fraud. Logic may then lead us to one of three conclusions: 1) There is no perfect partner for us and we must come to terms with this reality as best we can; 2) We have failed in the search for a perfect soul mate through some personal flaw and/or conditions beyond our control and must make the best of this situation; or 3) We need to renew our search and hope to use better judgment next time. If we stay in the relationship, no matter what our conclusions, the myth of the perfect partner often causes us to withdraw a small part of ourselves just in case our real soul mate does someday come along.

Actually, at the level of the soul, we are all by virtue of our common membership in the human race very much alike. The truth is that we are all soul mates with everyone else. Our differences are really only in the packaging. Qualities like age, education, physical and personality characteristics distinguish us from one another on a superficial level. We can tinker with the packaging by learning new skills, curling our hair, or laughing on the outside while crying on the inside. The essential self however remains constant in each of us and differs from person to person primarily in how much each one of us expresses and to whom.

As we saw in Chapter Four, theoretically anyone can fall in love with anyone else, because real love is an experience from our own essence of another's essential self. Practically, whom we allow ourselves to love depends to a great extent on that person's packaging and how well it fits with our own ideas about love. Our needs for a certain type of person or relationship in our life at the time we fall in love also has a great influence on whom we allow ourselves to love.

For example, a person may look appealing because he

or she is attractive according to our preferences and prejudices. Generally, we will be attracted to people who are most like us or like the people we have known and liked in the past, or people we have decided are appealing because of media propaganda or some other experience. We may be further attracted because the person exhibits certain personality characteristics that we enjoy such as being fun loving, intellectual, or strong and decisive. We may draw closer because we intuitively sense that he or she will be able to meet certain needs we have, possibly for understanding or playfulness. Usually we sense at a deep and often unconscious level certain similarities in this person to others we have loved in the past. Invariably, these similarities are both positive and negative. Equally inevitable is the surprise we feel when the negative aspects of the person become apparent in the relationship.

It is important to note that what we consider to be the negative aspects of the people we love are just as crucial to our relationship as their positive characteristics. We are attracted to these negative characteristics, although usually unconsciously, because it is the opportunity to learn to love just precisely these characteristics that is essential to developing the ability to expand the experience of love throughout our life. Why this is so will become more clear in later chapters.

Everyone we ever will or could love will exhibit a combination of qualities that will be both appealing and appalling to us as we grow to know one another better. Some relationships we might form will definitely be more likely to be more pleasant and successful than others. This, however, has more to do with the interactive effect of our individual personality characteristics, especially our beliefs, behavior, and interpersonal skills, than on the rightness or wrongness of our initial attraction for one another. All relationships hold the possibility for a deep experience of love for one another, but no relationship is guaranteed success solely on the basis of how much or how well we love.

Myth Number Two: True Love Solves All Problems. The belief that with time and love all problems will eventually wither away probably causes more personal distress and interpersonal conflict and ineffectiveness than any other relationship myth. It is not the function of love to solve problems. In fact, love is more likely to create problems. It is sure to create challenges and to raise questions and issues in a relationship. As long as we believe that true love solves problems and define our love as therefore not "true" when problems do arise, then we will miss the real benefit of loving feelings as motivators to seek workable ways to meet the inevitable challenges of a love relationship.

One of the most basic intrinsic benefits of any experience is the element of opportunity to learn more about one's self and the world that inevitably exists in it to one extent or another. Whether an experience has been fun, profitable, entertaining, satisfying or debilitating, painful and humiliating, it always holds the potential for learning new perspectives and acquiring wisdom. This is particularly true of intimate love relationships. The closer we grow to one another, the better we know each other, the more we give of ourselves and experience life together, the more opportunity we will have to experience and observe contradictions in our individual belief systems and our actual experience of the world. The intensity of our feelings for one another causes a corresponding discomfort with the other's differing values, beliefs, and behavior. In order to become comfortable enough with one another to maintain our closeness, we must struggle through our differences to mutually acceptable resolutions. In the process, we have a great opportunity to learn the greater truth that is inherent in the piece of life's puzzle each one of us has within his or her individual frame of reference. Simply practicing this skill within the highly emotionally charged context of a love relationship strengthens the ability to do this in other less threatening areas of life. Regardless of all our fears, the process of expanding one's frame of reference is the vehicle for human evolution, a process that is constantly taking place on the individual and personal level. The difficulty is that we may believe giving up one position and looking for a new, mutually acceptable point of view could diminish us and leave us weaker or less independent or indicate a lack of character and autonomy. Actually, doing this is a deeply strengthening, fundamentally fortifying act. Although it is hard and sometimes painful to give up dearly held beliefs and opinions, responses and reactions, if we are to live life to the fullest, it is necessary to evaluate and discard any part of us that does not support growth and well-being in all situations. Intimate relationships give us an arena in which to challenge our belief systems and liberate ourselves from the ones that do not serve us. The more we resist these challenges, the more problems we will experience in relationships. The more we can confront the challenges, the greater our opportunity to grow. It is not love, however, that will solve these problems but our mutual good will, openness to other points of view, and our communication, listening, and problem-solving skills. Fortunately, none of these necessary ingredients are magic or mysterious; they can be developed and learned if the desire is there along with the willingness to suspend beliefs and embrace change.

Myth Number Three: Our Feeling For One Another Will Never Change. When we first fall in love it seems inconceivable that we should ever feel negatively toward this person who seems to embody all that is good and beautiful. Our experience, however, shows that it is usually not too long before we get close enough to begin to fear rejection, withdraw some of our enthusiasm, and thus initiate a trend in the relationship that will highlight our differences and fears. Feelings can change dramatically at this point. This is not the only time our feelings will change but just the first of many both dramatic and unremarkable changes of feeling lovers will experience together.

Of course, we all understand that we will sometimes feel irritable, angry, tired, bored as well as excited, contented, or tender with one another. Moment by moment, day by day our feelings fluctuate; they arise and pass to be replaced by new feelings in response to the momentary conditions of the environment, our own thoughts and physical condition, and other less easily identified stimuli. This is not what we mean when we say our feelings will never change. What we are referring to is a more basic and sustained experience of loving attitudes and intentions, of good will and openness to our partner, of pleasure in his or her company, and a sense of lack or loss when we are apart.

The fact is that these more basic feelings can change as well in one of two directions. Over time, as lovers experience each other under a variety of conditions and confront life's ongoing problems together, love may become richer and more fulfilling and may seem at times to be lost forever. These differences arise not so much out of the nature of the problems that partners face as from how the problems are handled and resolved. An affair or a financial crisis may ruin one relationship, while for another couple such a situation can provide the basis for dialogue that ultimately results in a renewal of love and a strengthening of the partners' bond. Even the most effective and vital partnerships will have periods in which the feeling of deep abiding love has fled and the partners fear their love will never return.

The truth is that partners' feelings for one another will change regularly throughout the course of a long-term relationship and these changes will fluctuate between the poles of ever-deepening love and disinterest or actual dislike. These cycles in feelings are only indicators of how well we are doing together in communicating about the ongoing process of change and growth that is part of all relationships. Many people needlessly waste energy worrying about fluctuations in the level of their feelings rather than systematically and effectively analyzing together what avenues are available to restore interest and harmony in mutually satisfying ways. Typically, partners will blame one another for any relationship difficulties, thereby opening the door to talking themselves into terminating the relationship rather than looking for the mutual opportunities for growth that exist in the situation. The first step in a positive process for handling an apparent loss of love is to accept the truth that changes in feeling are a part of any deep and vital relationship and that a period of discomfort with one another does not mean that love is lost forever. In fact, if handled with confidence and mutual good faith it may precede a renewal of transcendent love.

Myth Number Four: True Love Provides an Oasis of Peace in a Cruel and Stressful World.   While it is true that there are times when an intimate relationship will provide a source of sustenance and nurturing for partners who feel beset by problems at work, with children, or in other areas of life, it is a myth that the relationship always *should* provide this kind of support or that this is its highest function. When we strive to develop a relationship primarily as a haven or refuge from life's difficulties, we are placing severe limits on the possibilities the relationship offers. In doing so we may also be building a placid façade that will ultimately result in sapping the life energy from our interactions together.

It is unrealistic to require that partners always interact with gentleness and total understanding. Sometimes we will not understand each other, nor will we feel tender and supportive at every moment. To pretend attitudes that are not real only alienates us; making a habit of alienating behavior undermines intimacy. This is not to say that there are not times when personal feelings need to be set aside or impulsive behavior modified because of a partner's individual problems or situational stress. Caring for another sometimes requires a sensitivity to short-term situations that are outside the control of either partner.

Over the long term, however, a vigorous relationship is

one that can be trusted to support an honest expression of feelings and an active raising of concerns as well as appreciation on the part of both partners. The highest goal of an intimate relationship, if it is to continue to meet the needs for a real and vital love between partners, must be a continuing and active effort on the part of both partners to keep one another up to date on the flow of feelings (positive and negative) and issues each one experiences in his or her personal life and within the relationship. It is in this way that the relationship can most effectively act as a supportive base for the individual lives of the couple. When this condition exists there will always be at least one person in the world who can be trusted to give an honest response and who is committed to working out differences in ways that benefit both parties. Simply knowing this can be done within the highly emotional context of an intimate relationship, can open the possibilities of more effective problem solving in other areas of life. Feeling free to share positive feelings with a loved one can have the effect of freeing people to be more positive with others. Children, work associates, and social relationships may reap the benefit of a habit of spontaneous and straightforward expressions of feeling. We can learn together how to criticize with caring and how to express caring without manipulation or seductiveness.

Myth Number Five: Love Is Blind.   The idea that love is blind is used to explain the very common experience of discovering that yesterday's perfect love has become today's clay idol. It is upsetting, sometimes painfully so, to learn that the one who seemed to be the embodiment of truth, beauty, and compassion can also be surly, have disagreeable habits, and not always act with fairness or consideration. When lovers begin to discover one another's less desirable human characteristics there is often an initial sense of betrayal followed by a period of wondering how it is possible to be "taken in" so completely by another person. Lovers tend to chastise one another for being dishonest and themselves for being foolish and gullible. For some it is but a short step to disillusionment with love and a growing cynicism about human relationships.

Of course, every lover puts his or her best foot forward in the initial stages of a relationship and often either unconsciously or deliberately does not expose the other to some aspects of self that might result in rejection. Also, people in love are unusually happy, and it may take some time before every day stress begins to effect them in the ordinary ways. When this experience of daily life does begin to return to normal, they will behave differently than they did during the euphoric period of falling in love. Transcendent love is us at our best, and when the experience passes we can look quite different to one another.

For this reason the unpleasant surprises and sometimes nasty shocks we experience as we learn more about one another need to be seen as normal and ordinary experiences rather than a result of duplicity or folly. If we can learn to accept in advance that any potential partner will have human weaknesses as well as strengths, then we will not need to waste energy blaming ourselves or one another when the weaknesses become apparent. It is not helpful to argue with reality. Reality simply exists to teach us about life. The real folly is in resisting the opportunities to learn.

At a deeper level, the truth is that we do know a great deal more about one another than we are consciously aware. Lovers have a deep intuitive sense of one another that encompasses the potential problem areas in the relationship as well as the positive things they can give to one another. This is not to say we are aware of one another's hidden bad habits or unpleasant behavior patterns, but we do tend to choose one another for the issues we can raise for each other as well as the support and love we can give. Once we recognize and accept this truth, we can begin to understand that the perfect love is not a love without problems but one that presents the perfect challenges. These are those challenges we need most in order to grow to become the energetic, creative, and compassionate people that we are at our very best. Falling in love gives us the experience of a goal we can strive for as growing and developing adults, and the means by which to achieve it. It is by working out the issues that arise that we may learn to be all we can be, both individually and together.

Myth Number Six: Opposites Attract. Another way we have of explaining disillusionment in love is the theory that while opposites attract like the poles of a magnet, it is similarities in personality and character that make a relationship work. If this were true all love would be doomed from the start, and we would be much better off using a computerized system for the selection of a mate or giving up the hope for satisfaction in long-term relationships entirely.

It is true that people often choose a partner at least partly because that person seems to have qualities and strengths that the other has not developed. For example, an indecisive person might like the other's ability to make plans and follow through on them; a very emotional person may be attracted to one who always remains calm and serene; a shy person may be drawn to someone who seems comfortable in any social situation. It is also true that often these initially attractive differences create problems later on in the relationship: a very socially active partner may want people around more often than a shy person can tolerate; decisiveness may look like stubborn inflexibility and pigheaded tenaciousness in some situations; calm serenity can begin, in time, to seem like indifference and even rejection to an emotionally expressive person.

Usually, however, when partners begin to look beneath the surface of conflicts created by what seem to be differences in personality, they discover that what they saw to be opposite characteristics are only different ways of handling similarly experienced problems. A shy person and an extremely outgoing person may only be exhibiting the ways that each one has learned to deal with the discomfort and fears they feel about being close to another. While the shy one withdraws, the social one has learned to hide fears and keep people distant with a barrage of small talk and a whirlwind of activity. The conflict created in relationships by seemingly opposite characteristics is often only an invitation to look deeper into the problem and to see it in a new way. In this sense intimates who appear to be opposites on the surface are really providing a mirror for one another to learn more about themselves and discover new alternatives for coping with problematic areas of life.

Myth Number Seven: True Love Is Exclusive Love. The time-honored test of true love is that it is a unique experience, a feeling each of us can have with only one person. This belief is constantly being contradicted in experience. As a result we have invented a vast array of complex theories about the nature of love. We have also developed a number of concepts to help us distinguish between true love and other kinds of feelings we have for one another. We may therefore label a brief affair infatuation or call our feelings for someone we view as an inappropriate love object "chemistry." When a relationship ends we may decide that it was only romantic passion that brought us together or that we were "in love with love" and not one another.

This belief can raise serious issues both for people who are enjoying a rewarding love relationship as well as for those whose relationships leave something to be desired. The man who believes that he has married his true love and yet discovers that he has loving feelings for another woman must decide if this experience means that his love for his wife is not true love or if he is merely sexually attracted to the other woman. The woman who feels love for all of the several men she dates may conclude that she is ficklehearted and incapable of the depth of character necessary for experiencing true love.

The more we experience love in our lives, the more confused we may become about what true love might be and how to know it when we find it. It is ironic that the most loving people are often the most confused and upset about their feelings. If true love means one and only one person, then those who allow themselves to feel love for many people can easily persuade themselves that they are immature, superficial, and incapable of experiencing real love.

The truth about love is that all love is real. Call it what we may, love is love. Whether the experience lasts a moment or a lifetime has nothing to do with its validity or reality. All of love is an experience of our own essence mirrored in the essence of another. It is possible to have this experience with anyone at any time. We may feel a flash of love in the presence of someone we normally do not even like. We may experience love for people we consider to be the wrong age, or the wrong sex, or who are otherwise inappropriate as a relationship partner. We can fall in love with a whole room of people at the same time. The feeling of love itself is nothing but good and beautiful. It is only our beliefs and the decisions we make based on these beliefs that create problems.

Hand in hand with the belief that true love is exclusive is the conviction that if we love someone we must have a relationship with that person. This would make sense if it were a fact that there is only one true love. In reality, however, this belief serves to obscure the true nature of love even further. One result is that we unconsciously place limits on our feelings for people that do not appear to be potential relationship partners. This results in us missing some opportunities to have pleasant feelings about other people. If this were the only cost however, the problem would not be severe. Simply missing out on some nice feelings is the least of the penalties we pay by limiting our ability to love. The more inappropriate we believe a love relationship with a particular person or group of people to be, the stronger the barriers we must erect against the possibilities of positive feelings. Thus we develop prejudice against people of different racial or cultural backgrounds and discomfort with touching or tenderness between members of the same sex. Potential love becomes uneasiness, dislike, and even hatred, which in turn limits even further capabilities of expressing love to those close to us. The more we limit love, the less we find of love in the world. Its absence is filled with fear, hatred, and strife—all the qualities that are a manifestation of the absence of love, as cold is the absence of heat.

At the root of all this confusion is simply a lack of awareness of what forms the basic bonds that unify two people in an enduring intimate partnership. If it is not "true love" that makes a relationship special and we are no longer tied to one another by economic necessity, then we must wonder what keeps us together and why.

It is the possibility for ever richer and more varied experiences of love that can be found only in an intimate, deeply trusting alliance that is the adhesive that still holds us together once the myths about love are exploded and practical considerations left behind. Two people who love one another, who view each other as equals, and are committed to the growth and well-being of both partners and of their relationship have a unique opportunity. They have a chance to discover together the underlying unity in their apparent differences and to create mutually their own version of the joyous dance that reflects the essence of unification of polarities. Deep and transcending love is only one of the by-products of this process. Mastering of this aspect of unity leads to profound changes in the individuals' relationships with all areas of life. It opens the door to a special kind of creativity, one that is exhibited moment by moment, day by day, in the humblest activities as well as the most consequential.

When love seems unsatisfying and relationships become a burden, it is wise to look for the beliefs that may be holding us back from a full experience and expression of feelings. There is no scarcity of love in the world other than the artificial scarcity we have created out of the myths and beliefs that obscure love's true nature. All of us, at a deep and intensely personal level, know that we are seeking love in many ways that may not appear at all related to love. Once we recognize that possessions, sex, the social whirl, accomplishments, and even marriage and children do not automatically fulfill our craving for love, we can begin to look for love where it really resides and to learn to express it within the contexts and in the ways that are most consistent with its true nature.

6

Where Is the Love?

Not long ago, one of our country's most prominent liberal politicians publicly denounced a scientific study into the nature of love, declaring that the American people do not want to know the facts about this magic feeling. Love, he insisted, should remain a mystery. Many people do prefer to think of love as an unfathomable experience, one that depends on factors outside our control. It can be upsetting to realize that love is an inner experience and that we ourselves erect the barriers that prevent us from having more love in our lives.

Fortunately, knowing more about love does not detract from its magic. In fact, this knowledge can give us hope that we may be able to learn ways to experience more of the magic that is our heart's desire. Realizing that each of us is in charge of our own loving feelings is a double-edged sword, however, since we do not really know how we stop ourselves from loving. We are more than a little afraid to hold ourselves accountable for our dissatisfactions with love. It is more comfortable to blame the behavior and attitudes of others for our complaints than to ask ourselves what we would have to change to feel satisfied in our love relationships.

We all know that change is difficult. Most of us have trouble keeping a New Year's resolution even for a few days. Many self-improvement projects are just as likely to fail as they are to succeed. If we discover that we must make some personal changes so that we may love more, we bring up the specter of fear of failure.

Handling this fear is the first hurdle we must cross. To do so we need to challenge our beliefs about change. Real change does not arise from consciously trying hard to be different. This tactic usually results in anxiety, guilt, and self-punishment. All of us have plenty of criticism in our lives already; we do not need to add our own voice to the voices and thoughts of others. Trying hard to change is uncomfortable and is just as likely to make things worse for us as to improve them.

Real change, the kind that takes place at the deepest level, involves understanding both the possibilities for growth in our lives and the ways in which we prevent ourselves from exhibiting all that we already are. As children we believed that once we reached physical maturity all our growing was behind us. Somewhere in the late teens or early twenties we would step across an invisible line that separates growing children and adolescents from fully formed and stable adults. At this point real life would begin. Most of us are now recognizing, and research in social psychology is confirming, that while the body stops growing during the teen years, it is still possible and most likely imperative to continue to grow intellectually, emotionally, and spiritually as adults. Rather than being a time of stability or even organic smooth change and growth, adulthood can bring even stronger emotional conflicts and more confusing challenges than puberty. Recognizing this reality is the first step toward taking charge of our growth as adults. The biggest difference between our growth as a child and as an adult is that now we are in charge. We have lost the comfort of following the directions of our older and wiser caretakers, but we have gained the opportunity to develop our own wisdom and strength.

It is helpful in understanding the process of adult growth and development to take a look at what is going on in the entire life cycle of each of us. All of us come into the world with a similar and yet unique set of potential qualities. These qualities exist in us at the time of birth. When we are born we look something like this:

Each of us has many, many more qualities in potential at birth than those listed. Most of them are shared by all of us. How completely we develop them and how we exhibit them depends upon the environment we were born into and our experience of that environment as we grow. A child whose spine is injured at birth may never walk even though he or she has all the muscles and mental processes necessary for walking. The nerve injury will prevent the mental messages from reaching the muscles. Fortunately most children learn to walk; when they begin will depend on the strength of the walking urge. What their characteristic adult walking style will be can depend on many factors. A chronically depressed person may walk slowly and ponderously. A childhood injury may result in a lifelong limp. I patterned my own gait after a description of the fictional detective Nancy Drew's walking style until teasing by my peers motivated me to drop the habit of bouncing along like a kangaroo.

A few children are born with very special talents. If conditions are right these children develop into child prodigies in music or mathematics. For such a person, many other potentials may be ignored or left underdeveloped while all energies are directed to the area of special skill.

For most of us, however, the urges to bring out all of our different qualities are fairly well balanced. We will all feel a desire to develop our intelligence, our talents, our creativity, and our ability to feel and to love. We begin to express these qualities even as very small children. As we interact with the things, events, and people that make up our early childhood environment, we begin to learn what types of expression are associated with feeling good and comfortable and what types leave us feeling worse off than when we started. As we saw in Chapter Two, we draw conclusions and begin to develop the behavior and attitudes that will result in our characteristic roles through this interaction with our environment. And we do it very early in life. Many child psychologists assert that one's basic personality is formed by the time he or she is five or six. The rest of life is spent refining this basic personality. So, at five or six we look like this:

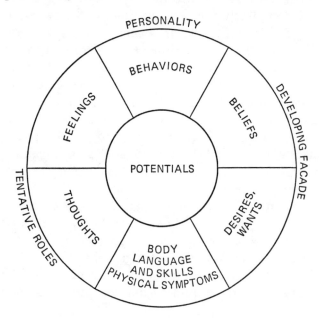

This is a picture of our developing personality. All the qualities we are born with are still with us, but now they are both expressed and inhibited by a set of beliefs, feelings, behaviors, physical expressions and sensations, wants, etc., that we have learned in order to interact with the world around us effectively. Each of us is finding the best possible way to express our basic qualities in our own particular environment, and we are also beginning to develop the personality characteristics that are consistent with the level of ease or difficulty we are finding our expression to be. In the process we are growing more unique and differentiated from one another. This process of differentiation will continue as we grow. It is the result of varying memories, decisions, and experiences we have in life and ways that we develop to deal with the problems of being who we are in the world that seems inconsistent in its response to us.

As adults our personality looks like this:

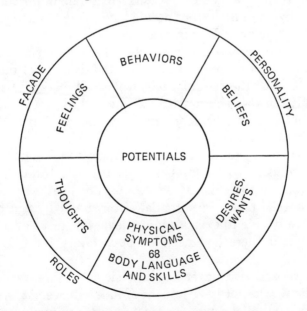

At our core all the potentials we were born with still exist. Many of them have been actualized to one extent or another through the various aspects of our personality. We can all walk, talk, smile, and think. How well we do these things depends on what our experience in life has been. A person who sits behind a desk all day walks just as well as anyone else, but he or she may not run very well unless a special effort is made through exercise and training to build muscles, lungs, and the cardiovascular system. The potential for running, however, still exists. The same is true with thinking. All of us think, but the nature of our thinking is determined by the training our minds have received and by how we have learned to cope with the beliefs, assumptions, and feelings that can cloud clear thinking. Some psychologists postulate that we use less than 10 percent of the mental power available to us. Our minds are developed but not to the fullest extent of our potential.

In adulthood, individual differences abound. As we look around at one another, it sometimes seems that the differences among us are paramount. Adults are often quite surprised when they learn that other people have thoughts and feelings just like their own. This is specially true about those feelings we do not like and consequently do not often speak of— insecurities, fears, and anxieties top the list. Yet at our core, at the level of the essential self, we are all markedly similar. It is only our interaction with the unique life experiences and the qualities of the decisions and responses we have all made that differentiate us.

Imagine a Mozart who had no piano and no opportunity to hear music as a child. The urge to create through music was strong in the child Mozart even in his earliest years. He had a special talent in potential at birth and by age five he was already able to exercise it at a level few of us ever reach. But what if there had been no opportunity for him to do this?

If Mozart had never heard music as an infant or young child he would not have known of its existence. At the same time he would have experienced an undefined yet strong urge to express the talent he had within. Having neither the experience of music nor the thought process and skills to identify his undefined urges, he would have become increasingly upset and frustrated. At some level he would have known there was something wrong, and yet he would have not been able to do anything about it. Instead he would randomly try various ways to express his energy. We might imagine him banging on pots and glasses to make sounds and in the process breaking things and giving his mother a sick headache. Perhaps she might have removed him to a safer place and, thinking she was doing the right thing, surrounded him with safe, unbreakable things that would not make any noise. Poor Mozart's frustration level would be increased. He might become unmanageable or at some point give up in total frustration and retreat into autism.

Fortunately for the world, this did not happen to Mozart. But in milder ways this does happen to all of us. We need to see and feel the thing we are trying to express in order to know how to do it. If people talk to us we will learn language and begin to communicate. If people hold and kiss us, understand our feelings, and respond to our needs with kindness, we will begin to learn something about expressing love. If we reach out in love with childish clumsiness to a tired and irritable caretaker, we may learn something else that conflicts with the learnings we have had. What we decide to do with this conflict depends on us and what we have already seen and experienced. We may redouble our efforts to express love, we may withdraw, we may respond out of our frustration by crying or having a temper tantrum. As the process of action and reaction between our need for expression and the response of our environment continues, our individual personalities are shaped and strengthened. Our apparent differences become more varied, yet underneath all those apparent variations the same constellation of characteristics are seeking expression in each of us.

As we grow older our choices for expression expand.

When we reach adulthood and move out of the family's sphere of influence, we assume more and more dominion over our expression. We enter new environments that challenge us in different ways than our childhood environment did. At each stage of adulthood we are having experiences that offer us the opportunities to examine how well we have succeeded in expressing our inner qualities and to find new, creative, and possibly more satisfying ways of doing this.

Old habits die hard. We have seen in Chapter Two how the frame of reference we develop early in life creates self-fulfilling prophecies and operates to keep us within the established patterns. Each time we move into a new environment with its different rules, we open ourselves to an experience of inner conflict. The more different the new environment from our past experience, the more conflict we may feel. At the same time, the opportunity to find more satisfying ways to express some of our qualities is enhanced. How well we do with this depends on how well we accept and understand the differences and how well the new environment supports us in our process of sorting out inner conflict and learning new forms of expression. Whether the climate is gentle or harsh, new learning can take place. The process is most pleasant in a gentle environment, but some real consequences to not learning the new requirements must be present for us to be willing to change at all.

An example all of us can share is the process of leaving home for the first time and embarking on adulthood alone. Whether we chose college, a job, the military service, or travel and adventure, all of us were confronted with the necessity to learn a great many new things in a short period of time in order to succeed. We had to learn the rules of the new situation, whether they included being on time for class or work, or involved fending for ourselves on the road and finding a safe place to sleep at night. We had to test the skills we had already gained in life against the requirements of the new situation. How well could we manage time for studying, become efficient in following orders with good grace, or learn to keep house and be a loving companion? If new skills were needed, could we develop them and did we want to make the effort? Our values were questioned by exposure to new people and new ideas. Dealing with issues of sex, honesty, violence, responsibility, freedom, and the meaning of life are all part of a young person's experience upon leaving home for the first time. How well we handle these first new challenges as adults will have a great impact on how well we will be able to respond to the still unknown issues and conflicts later in life.

It is at this point that folk wisdom and traditional research deserts us. The child is safely launched into career and/or marriage. He or she is now an adult who will lead an adult life more or less successfully. Although it remains to be seen how each individual life will turn out, the groundwork has been laid and only time will tell whether the newly hatched adult will have the good fortune and the strength of character to make it in life. Every man for himself and may the best man win. Whether the prize is material success, intellectual achievement, or raising a model family, we are on our own.

It is heartening to see some changes in our thinking about adulthood and some new efforts being made today to try to uncover the underlying themes and conflicts of adult life. All of us can take some comfort from the new research into adult growth and development. At the very least it shows us that we are neither alone nor totally unique in our response to the parade of issues that confront us as adults. Beyond that, however, new findings about the adult life cycle point to some dramatically different ways of looking at growth and change in adulthood that can help us discover ways to enhance our ability to grow creatively and productively.

Normal adult development seems to be characterized by relatively brief periods of tumultuous inner conflict followed by longer periods of integration and activity. The crisis periods occur approximately once every decade and can last from one to about five years. The crisis usually begins with feelings of dissatisfaction, uselessness, and confusion. It seems as if the life has gone out of living. The spark and the spice is gone. Things that were once interesting and challenging become a bore. We may wonder how or why we ever got interested in the first place. A period of life crisis is often initiated by reaching an important goal or the realization that a cherished goal will not be reached. Business success in the early forties is the event that initiates what we have come to call mid-life crisis for many men. Even more men at that age, however, face the necessity of recognizing that they will fail to reach the top of the ladder in business. This is the experience that heralds a period of turmoil for many.

Whatever the initiating event and regardless of whether any particular dramatic event marks the beginning of a crisis period, the feelings we experience are strikingly similar. Anxiety, depression, emotional and mental confusion, frustration, and even despair are common feelings. We begin to question the meaning of life and our own lives in particular. Joy has fled, happiness seems an illusion, and we are lost and floundering. At this point panic may set in and cause a variety of reactions. Some people exercise enormous will power and set about doing what they have always done with more determination. On the outside they look as if they are doing pretty well. They attend the same parties, go to work as usual, and continue to play the same roles with competence. Something inside, however, is not the same. They know it, and others can sense it. Whatever zest and vitality they may have felt when they were younger has deserted them. These are the people who lead lives of quiet desperation and who may find some solace in alcohol, drugs, or compulsive activity.

Another extreme reaction to panic occurs in those who suddenly decide to change everything about the life they were leading. These people have reached the conclusion that the structures of work, leisure, and relationships they have built up around them are at fault. They may suddenly flee their families and/or throw over their careers. If unmarried, they may decide to marry; if they have been drifting in work they may decide to commit themselves to a cause or a vocation. Various possibilities present themselves at different times in life. Those chosen depend on what the individual has already done in life and what the possibilities for fulfillment look like now. Some new choices may be excellent, others may be devastating. In any event, the person who responds to panic by drastic change will face a period of very hard work in the following integration process. Everything that has been built up may have been sacrificed in the change. New structures must replace them. Other people may have been hurt and damaged in the process. The consequences of this can color an entire lifetime no matter how beneficial the choice.

Some people can neither find the will power to continue leading the same life nor the courage to make a dramatic change. If the inner conflict is extreme, they may withdraw from life or begin to exhibit symptoms of severe mental distress. Many come through such an experience strengthened and renewed; some never really return. For most, however, the period of panic is somehow weathered. They respond in less extreme ways and find some kind of inner or outer support for experiencing the panic to completion. Friends, family counseling, religion, and inner reflection can all offer some support, depending on the individual. Once panic has passed, a mental sorting-out process begins. Each crisis period causes us to assess the totality of our lives and to begin to recognize and accept parts of ourselves that we had ignored in the previous growth cycles. Those aspects of ourselves that we learned to put away as children and did not actualize as young adults begin to assert themselves and ask for recognition. The super-rational, clear-thinking man begins to experience emotions he never dreamed were part of himself. The supporting, nurturing mother finds she wants a life of her own outside of the family. Interests change, new goals emerge, and some adjustment in life style and activities are sought to incorporate new understandings. This begins the integration period to be followed by yet another crisis, more or less severe, depending on how the previous crisis was resolved and how much of the essential self remains unseen and unactualized.

Healthy adult development does not preclude or prevent life crises. These crises are an integral and necessary part of growth and change. We can modify the pain and increase our chances of beneficial resolution by understanding what is at issue, but we can never avoid crises entirely. Nor should we want to, since developing the ability to be and express all that we truly are is a direct result of effectively resolving the issues raised at crisis points.

As an adult grows older and experiences and resolves life crises in healthy ways, he or she begins to look like this:

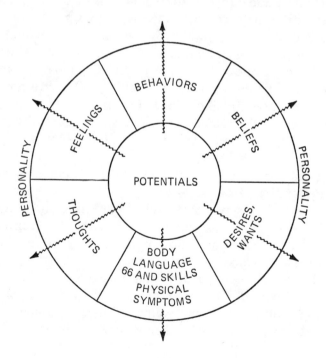

There is more communication between the inner urges and the outer personality. The individual feels more comfortable with him/herself and less conflicted over thoughts, feelings, behaviors, and beliefs that seem contradictory, ineffective, or do not fit with experience. More of the inner potentials, therefore can find expression in the world. The individual is more open to the responses of the environment and thus can find increasingly more satisfying and effective behavioral expressions of the essential self. Wants and desires are more consistent with the deepest inner needs for growth and the enhancement of those qualities and characteristics shared by all of us. As the individual expresses more of these qualities in the world, he or she falls into alignment with the deepest needs of other people and society as a whole. The contribution such a person makes in life, whether in work, in the family, or in social interaction, grows increasingly creative, personally satisfying, and effective. Such people seem a little bit unusual to those that know them well, since they do not seem to share the same worries and concerns for formality and structure that the rest of us have learned over a lifetime of social conditioning. Yet somehow things seem to go well in their lives. They radiate a kind of peace and confidence that is arresting. Most of these people go about their lives quietly and do not come to our attention. Generally, they are willing to pretend they are like the rest of us in social situations— they follow polite form, show empathy and compassion for the concerns of others whether or not they share them, and generally make themselves likable if a trifle distant and self-contained. We are likely to overlook them and thus miss learning some of the important lessons about living they could share with us.

Abraham Maslow devoted his life to the study of such people. He called them self-actualizers. The conviction that these unusual people are what we all could and can be, if we only knew how, permeates his works. He identified such historical figures as Ghandi and Lincoln as possible or partial self-actualizers. Other psychologists followed and expanded on his ideas in a search for ways to enhance the possibilities for more people to grow to self-actualization. They learned that such conditions as acceptance, love, understanding, and honest communication among people promotes growth toward greater wholeness and lessens inner conflict and anxiety. When these conditions are present in a relationship, whether it be among friends, marriage partners, or a therapist and client, change occurs in all the people involved. It seems that the more supportive and loving the environment can be, while at the same time providing people with a clear picture of the realities of conflicting needs and interests, negative feelings and ineffective behaviors, the more people were able to take in all the information and see their own problems and conflicts in a new light. Under these conditions change became desirable and almost effortless instead of seeming difficult or dangerous. Instead of trying hard to overcome bad habits and negative attitudes, people were transcending their inner barriers to change, and as they did so, problems were resolved or fell away.

Real change—effective and growth-promoting change—does not involve applying a new set of rules, consciously substituting a new behavior for an old one, or developing a new role to set on top of all the old ones we have played. Real change grows out of the experience of seeing how the personality we have developed over the years obscures some important qualities in ourselves that we need to express in order to feel whole and complete. Real change means knowing that every conflict we experience, every negative emotion we feel, every difficult situation we confront is an invitation to find out more about how we have hidden parts of our essential self. Each weakness or fault we can find in ourselves (and in others as well) is only an incomplete and distorted expression of an inner strength that has not been acknowledged. A high percentage of our thoughts, feelings, and beliefs are simply ways that served us as children to mediate between inner urges and outer environment, but may now get in the way of our growth as adults. Once we can acknowledge the possibility that the inner potentials that make up the essential self are real and are present in us, and once we can begin to understand how and why we have stopped ourselves from expressing these qualities as fully as we might, then we have taken an important step in taking charge of our own individual process of growth and change. By doing so, we enhance the possibility of achieving full self-actualization for ourselves and promoting optimum growth toward wholeness in those dear to us.

All of us who have ever been in love have an idea of what self-actualization would be like for us. For most lovers, that period of transcendent love shines brightly in memory. Instead of wistfully resigning ourselves to the fact that this once-in-a-lifetime experience is behind us, we can see that what we felt then was only a foretaste of what lies ahead. The joy, the peace, the sense of harmony and beauty that are part of the transcendent love experience can be part of the daily experience of those of us willing to commit ourselves to the journey back to the essential self—that part of ourself that is love and is always loving. There is no greater adventure in life than the unfolding of this deeper, more basic and yet transcendent self. The time to start is any time you wish. It is never too early nor too late. The place to start is closest to home, and the person to start with is yourself.

7

Removing Internal Barriers to Transcendent Love

Kathy arrived at her weekly counseling session with a gift. It was a large poster showing a very battered, worn, and apparently exhausted rag doll sprawled in a corner. The caption read: "The truth shall set you free . . . but first it will make you miserable." Kathy handed me the poster with a wry smile. "This is how I feel right now," she said. "When I started all this changing I knew it would be hard, but I didn't think it would be *this* hard.

Kathy had a point. The process of change can be slower than we wish and often is full of snags and rough spots. Often we may experience pain that we do not wish to feel. We know the pain would go away for now if we would retreat, and it is a real temptation to do so at times. Kathy herself had been at the point of leaving therapy several times. Each time we would go over the advantages and disadvantages she saw. Always she came back to the same points. She *could* end the process of self-examination and behavior change that she had begun, but only at the cost of giving up on some very important relationships. Even though she knew she would survive and in some ways feel better if she left these relationships, this did not feel right to her. She could see that there was a good chance her interpersonal problems could be solved if her determination to do so was strong. She had also had enough life experience to realize that the same problems she faced in these relationships were likely to arise again in any new relationship she would develop. Kathy kept on despite her discouragement. Eventually she felt confident enough in her strength to leave therapy and continue growing on her own. The last time I saw her she described her new relationship with a stepdaughter (a relationship that had once been full of violent anger), so beautifully that it brought tears to my eyes.

Kathy's growing process is not finished. She knows that she has a lot of work left to do before she is comfortable with herself and her life. But she is beginning to reap some of the rewards of growth and finds the pain that arises from time to time is not as discouraging as before. What's more, she has concrete evidence from her own experience that personal change is possible and that she can take charge of that change.

Many people who speak and write about personal change and growth sound as if the process were as easy as whipping up an omelet. If you have the right ingredients and a good sense of timing, there's nothing to it. Their words, meant to be encouraging, often have the opposite effect. We try the techniques they suggest, and if we are not instantly changed we become even more discouraged about ourselves and about the possibility that things can ever be different for us.

Regardless of our discouragement or our optimism, however, the truth is that we *can* change our experience of life. Whether we want better relationships, more sense of personal accomplishment, greater vocational satisfaction, or more love in our lives, the possibilities are there. Despite the fact that it is easier said than done, it still *can* be done. We, and we alone, have the choice to give up on our lives, wait until external conditions are just right, or go ahead and take charge of our own growth and change right now. The processes and problems discussed in this chapter apply to all the changes we might desire and all of the issues and difficulties any of us may confront in our individual lives. The examples used refer to love and relationships, since some of our greatest challenges and strongest needs lie in this area. Relationships are hard. If you can do relationships well, you can do anything.

The first step is understanding that there is a sense in which we have complete and total responsibility for everything we experience in life. The last step is really knowing with every fiber of your being that this is true. In between is hard work, perhaps some pain and anxiety, and the joys that come from growth. Of all the steps, however, the first one is probably the hardest. The reason for this lies in the frame of reference—that constellation of beliefs and assumptions about ourselves, others, and life that we discussed in Chapter Two. We saw how frame of reference is developed in early childhood out of decisions we have made based on our experience. We saw how the incomplete information and immature reasoning process of a young child could distort experience and result in inaccurate conclusions. We also saw how we might perpetuate inaccurate conclusions through selective attention and self-fulfilling prophecies.

Our frame of reference tells us in no uncertain terms that others and things outside of us are responsible for our feelings and problems. If we stub a toe, we know it would not have happened if the chair leg had not been where we were walking. If we feel angry at our spouse for harsh words and irresponsible actions, we are absolutely sure that we would feel fine if they had not done or said what they did. Frame of reference's most severe limitation is that it almost always skips over our own responsibility. If we had avoided the chair leg our toe would not have hit it. If our toe were not full of nerves and our nervous system not set up to experience pain, we would not have been hurt even if we had hit it. Similarly, we might have had a very large part in creating the situation where a spouse might speak harshly or behave irresponsibly. Maybe they are remembering times when they have been the recipient of harsh words or retaliating for last night's argument. Additionally, we ourselves would never feel angry about someone else's behavior unless our minds were conditioned to label our responses to criticism or being let down as angry feelings. We might just as easily have been conditioned to feel sad, scared, or even sympathetic and compassionate in the same situation. It does not matter a bit that "any person in their right mind" would have done the same thing under similar circumstances. Social approval for our feelings does not alter the fact that the options in any given situation are enormous and include, among others, feeling neutral. Reality cannot be determined by vote. No matter how much agreement we all find in the world for our frames of reference, it is still possible that things could be, and perhaps actually are, different.

Taking responsibility for our experience does not mean, however, feeling at fault. No matter what we think, feel, or do, we are neither right nor wrong. There are simply effective and pleasant or ineffective and unpleasant consequences that await us for feeling, thinking, and acting as we do. Taking responsibility implies looking for the underlying dynamics that support our experience, not being to blame for it. Anyone who has an unpleasant experience in life that they can neither leave nor change by direct action or simple request really has only one effective alternative left. That alternative is to take responsibility for the experience and to open up to a discovery of its meaning to us.

Humans have experienced torture, brutal imprisonment, walking over hot coals, and even lack of oxygen and have not only survived but have been transformed and enhanced by the experience. The situations that life brings to the vast majority of us are fortunately not nearly so severe. There is one similarity, however, in all of life's events, from the most mundane to the most bizarre and extreme. That is that there is a lesson to be learned if we will look for it. Our myths, legends, and stories affirm this truth over and over.

Each of us has a unique set of lessons to learn from life. Whether we travel the world or never leave our birthplace, life will bring us the precise situations that we need to experience in order to learn the lessons that apply to us. My client, Kathy, knew this when she decided to stay with her husband and stepchild. Dorothy realized the same truth upon returning to Kansas from the Land of Oz. We have the choice to embrace life's lessons or turn away from them. To grow toward wholeness, we must embrace them.

Taking responsibility, then, means understanding that our difficulties and problems are only indicators of the possibility of learning something important that can lead us into a more joyful and loving experience of life. Every time we experience a problem we are only experiencing a limitation we have placed on ourselves. If it is possible for humans to be buried alive or to walk over hot coals without injury, it is surely possible for us to uncover within ourselves the qualities that will promote more loving, creative, and passionate human relationships. We already have everything we need. It is only a matter of learning how to free ourselves from our self-imposed barriers.

The second step in removing the barriers to transcendent love is awareness.* No one would consciously continue to erect a barrier to leading a fuller, happier life if they could see it for what it was. Most of us continue to be unaware of our barriers because we have simply not looked at them or, if we have, we have learned to call them something else. This is our old friend frame of reference at work again. Selective attention allows us to ignore many things about ourselves that we do not have categories to explain. Our minds are at work continuously, seldom resting even in sleep. A constant stream of sentences, impressions, mental images and pictures,

---

* For a fuller explanation of what follows, see *How to Love Every Minute of Your Life,* by Gay Hendricks and Carol Leavenworth, Prentice-Hall, 1978.

words, and snatches of music are dancing through our thoughts, one after the other, sometimes in pairs or trios, all moving at the speed of thought. It would be impossible to process all these random mental phenomena, so by selective attention we do not let ourselves be consciously aware of the majority of them. Only the ones that pertain to the subject at hand and make some sense within our frame of reference are allowed an audience. For the rest, banishment to the subconscious mind to bounce around and perhaps emerge again as a slip of the tongue or a cleverly disguised symbolic dream.

The same can be said for feelings. At a very young age we learn to control and suppress certain feelings. We do this by ignoring the physical sensations associated with them and by tensing our bodies so as not to experience them. Gradually over time we can lose conscious awareness of the small nuances of feeling that arise and pass continually in response to a day's events. Only very strong, intense feelings will arrest our attention.

Thoughts and feelings are primary starting points in the search for internal barriers to love. People who ignore many of their thoughts and who have learned to suppress their feelings can reverse this tendency and grow more aware of their internal experience. Perhaps the easiest way is to take advantage of any routine activity or hiatus in the day to check in on what is going on inside. Washing dishes, driving the car, or waiting in the doctor's office provides the opportunity to stop pursuing the thoughts that occupy our mind and simply observe them as they pass through. After spending some time with thoughts, you can take a minute to check on your body. What are the physical sensations in each part of your body? Is there tension in the stomach, neck, or jaws? Do you have a headache, is your heart beating rapidly, and are your palms wet and clammy? What do these sensations tell you about your feelings right now? Name the feelings you are experiencing.

All our feelings can be categorized as stronger or weaker

varieties of fear, anger, sadness, joy, and excitement or combinations of these five. Using these basic feelings simplifies the
process of identifying emotions. All of these feelings are common human emotions that each of us may experience several
times a day. If you notice that you never seem to feel one
or two of them, you are probably not paying attention to
an important part of yourself. Keep watching for those feelings
with special attention.

Thoughts are closely associated with feelings. When our
bodies give us a clue that we are having a feeling or we experience tension and stress but we cannot name the feeling giving
rise to the discomfort, our thoughts come to our aid. Here
is a typical inner monologue that is full of feeling-related
thoughts:

I wish I had never met him! What kind of a person would be so rude and inconsiderate? Maybe I just won't be home when he calls.	anger
What if he doesn't call?	fear
That would be just like him.	anger
We've had so much fun together, I just can't understand why he'd do something like this.	sadness
How can I ever face my friends after the way he treated me so badly in front of them?	embarrassment (anger + fear)
What will I do with myself tonight? I get so lonely when he's not around.	sadness

Watching our thoughts for messages about feeling is very
important because many times we use thinking as a way to
control or overcome feelings. We can tell ourselves that we
just have to be more understanding instead of being aware
that we are angry. Often we blame other people for faults

and bad behavior when we are really feeling sad or scared that they will desert us. It can be interesting and enlightening to watch the way we have trained our minds to help us hide from feelings we do not want to acknowledge or experience. Unacknowledged feelings get in the way of love. It is impossible to feel very loving toward someone when we are harboring anger and fears that we ourselves do not even consciously recognize. Bringing these feelings to the level of consciousness is what practicing awareness is all about.

With time and attention anyone can gain greater awareness of internal experience and learn to make swift checks on thought and feeling even during periods of absorbing activity or stress. This kind of awareness automatically helps us to be more whole, because we have more information about ourselves and our reactions to various situations. Additionally, knowing as much as we can about our own thoughts and feelings enables us to take the next step in resolving barriers to love.

GIVING UP RESISTANCE AND INTEGRATING FEELINGS

We do not have awareness of many feelings because we are resisting them. Once we see a feeling and know that it is a part of us, we still often continue to resist a full experience of it. Many feelings are both uncomfortable physically and unacceptable within our belief systems. Strong men should not feel fear. Many women still feel uncomfortable with anger. Regardless of the recent loosening of attitudes about the appropriateness of certain feelings for each of the sexes, very few of us will ever see a man cry at a business meeting.

Our training for living has its deficiencies. We have learned to drive flimsy automobiles sixty miles per hour in heavy traffic, but we have never learned to handle many feelings comfortably or appropriately. We learn to ignore, suppress, deny, talk ourselves out of, control, and redirect feelings, but not to handle them directly. We can jog, play tennis, or have ulcers, but not get angry at the boss. Occasionally negative feelings slip out in other ways—forgetting appointments, spilling coffee on the boss's desk, or blowing up because dinner is late. For the most part, however, the watchword is control, not expression.

Giving up resistance to feelings does not imply irresponsibly acting them out. It means allowing ourselves to feel them completely and deeply. One of the most interesting things about feelings is that once we allow ourselves to feel them, they pass. Really feeling a feeling means experiencing it completely throughout the whole body. This takes some practice, but it can be done. That headache, sore neck, or tense stomach is only resistance to some kind of feeling. We try to contain it in one part of the body, because we believe that if it gets away from us, it will become uncontrollable or overwhelming. We only believe this because we do not see the difference between feeling and behavior. Having a feeling does not imply that we must *do* anything with it. We may choose, upon reflection, to share it at an appropriate time and place, but we are not required to do even this much with it. In fact, it is *resisted* feelings that are most likely to overwhelm us, because they build up over time. On the other hand, a feeling fully felt is a feeling that has passed out of our experience and will not come back to plague us in dreams, tensions, or unwanted behavior. Not resisting is the only way to gain real control over them. It is the way to removing a major barrier to the deeper qualities of love, compassion, and creativity that all of us possess. There is a simple process that many people have found to be an excellent way to learn how to stop resisting feelings. Once you have noticed a thought, a physical sensation, or some other indicator of the presence of a feeling and have named the feeling, do the following:

1. Locate the tension or sensation that is associated with the feeling in your body.

2. Allow yourself to picture the situation that gave rise to your feelings.

3. Let the feeling expand over your entire body. You may find that you want to cry or that your body shakes a little. Do not resist any sensation. You may notice yourself trying to tense against the feeling from time to time. By breathing deeply you can let go of the resistance and continue to let the feeling expand.

4. When you have opened up as much as you can, actively intensify the feeling. If you are trembling, shake harder. Whatever your experience, deepen it.

5. Once you have felt the feeling as deeply as possible, challenge your belief system by forgiving yourself and anyone else involved for your feeling.

6. Notice if new feelings arise. Often we have more than one feeling in any situation. We may be angry with a spouse and at the same time feel fearful that he or she no longer loves us and sad because we have had a fight. If new feelings do arise, repeat the process with them.

After a little practice with this process most people find they can go through it in a few seconds to two or three minutes. Doing this does not mean you will never feel that feeling again, but it does allow you to clear the air for now and not build up feelings that might come out inappropriately in the future.

My friend Martha used this process to handle some feelings that had been spoiling nearly every day for her. She had been staying up late every evening to finish an important project and then getting up at her usual time to fix breakfast for her husband Al before he left for work. She was groggy and tired but still wanted to spend that time with him. They had few quiet moments together, and they both cherished those times. However, almost every morning they found themselves fighting over some silly, inconsequential issue. Al would leave, slamming the door, and Martha spent most of the morning feeling miserable. They always made up later, laughing together over their foolishness, but the morning fights continued.

Martha decided to stop resisting her feelings and went through the process outlined above. The first few times she had some trouble really forgiving herself and Al, but she also learned some things about herself. She found that under her anger she was afraid that Al resented the time she put into her work even though she always put off working on her project until he was asleep so they could spend some time together in the evenings. Once she was able to experience the feelings fully and release them through forgiveness she felt better. Instead of dragging her down, her thoughts were free enough for her to do more of her work during the day. She also discussed her feelings with Al, a process that led to greater closeness between them. Within a week their morning fights had stopped and both Martha and Al were feeling more productive in their work and more loving toward one another than they had in weeks.

Martha's experience was exciting to her. She could see that, whether or not she and Al had reached an understanding, by integrating her feelings she would have felt better about both of them anyway. What actually happened illustrates how readily a problem between two people can be solved even when only one of them makes a change. If she and Al had continued to fight in the mornings, Martha could have gone further with the process and learned how to short-circuit her angry feelings on the spot and not participate in the argument. It is hard for one person to have a fight alone. Instead of being at the mercy of her own feelings and Al's, Martha was in charge of the situation. She enjoyed the feeling of personal strength that she gained from taking complete responsibility and confronting this problem directly.

Everyone can learn to integrate their feelings this way, thus gaining more control over their own lives. It is helpful, but not necessary, to begin with those feelings that are most easy to let go of anyway. Some feelings can take longer than others to release and may require several sessions over a period of days. This is especially true of old familiar feelings or those that have been building up for a long time. For especially difficult feelings, the help of a good counselor or psychotherapist can shorten the time it takes to integrate them.

FORGIVENESS

The act of self-forgiveness is an important part of integrating feelings and growing toward wholeness. Forgiving others is really just a part of forgiving oneself. They are two sides of the same coin. After all, if those we love are contemptible, what does that say about us? And by extension, what kind of a person holds a grudge against someone who does not matter to them anyway? Forgiveness is a necessary step to removing barriers to love. We cannot feel loving while we are embroiled in thoughts of fault, blame, and wrongness. These thoughts, whether directed at self or others, limit our alternatives and take energy away from simply living life.

Lack of forgiveness is a partner of belief. Our feelings are based on ancient need. Anger is a response to a threat that requires direct action against an aggressor. We feel we are being attacked and counterattack in order to save ourselves. Fear is a response to a threat that requires flight from the situation or some other preventive measure. Sadness is a response to loss. There are relatively few situations that we face today that involve real threat or loss. The great majority of the small fears, angers, and sorrows that we might experience in a day or a week of living are symbolic and are strongly tied to our beliefs and expectations. Even most of our strongest feelings are not a response to any real-life or property-threatening situation or actual loss. Most of us are aware that many of our worries come to nothing. As Mark Twain once said, "I am an old man and I have known a great many troubles, but most of them never happened."

Most anger reflects a belief that things should not be the way they are. Generally, these are things that we are either not willing or unable to change. Anger between intimates can sometimes bring change but more often results in more of the same. Our angry expressions can actually perpetuate and worsen behavior that we dislike in those closest to us. Grief is only constructive when it helps us leave our loss behind. In fact, entire systems of psychotherapy are built on the truth that most of our feelings arise out of beliefs or expectations that do not hold up in reality. The problem with many of these therapies is they reach the conclusion that because this is true, we should not feel the feelings we really do feel. This only perpetuates the problem and compounds the conflict.

Let's look at the example of Bill and Janet. Bill comes home three days in a row and retires behind the newspaper for the rest of the evening. Janet is depressed and vaguely uneasy by the second day. If she looked at her feelings she would see that she is feeling scared that he does not love her and sad because she thinks she has lost him. These feelings arise out of the belief that people who love each other are always glad to see one another and once love is gone, the marriage quickly follows. She also believes that love is very fragile and that it is hard for a woman to hold a man. In some ways she has even been expecting Bill to stop loving her. The fact is, Bill loves her very much: He is having serious business problems but believes a man should not burden his wife with such things. He also expects her to be upset if she finds out, since a real man, he believes, is always in charge of his affairs.

Janet asks Bill if he loves her. He says he does, but he will not explain his behavior. Now Janet is even more upset because she wants to believe him when he says he loves her— a wife always trusts her husband—but finds she cannot. This added conflict deepens her depression. Dinners are late and the housework is undone. The more she argues with herself about her feelings, the worse she feels. Bill notices, fears she has caught wind of the business situation, and grows even more tense and withdrawn. Two people who need each other's support in a challenging time have become estranged from one another. It may take days or weeks to work it out.

Both Bill and Janet have the ability to stop this cycle by integrating their feelings, forgiving one another, and suspending belief long enough to find out what is really going on. Most people who do this are surprised to discover that the truth can sometimes be very far from what they thought. Misunderstandings like the one Janet and Bill created are the stuff of drama and farce. We need less of this kind of drama in real life and more real understanding.

Our beliefs are a reflection of our frame of reference. None of us has the whole story and we all have distortions based on conclusions we drew from long-ago experiences. Many of our feelings are symbols pointing to our erroneous conclusions about life. They are helpful because they allow us to see limiting assumptions we have made so long ago that we could never actually remember making them. The major function of problems and our feelings about our problems is to allow us to see how we have limited ourselves so that we may have the chance to stop doing it. Once we open up even a small space in our armor of belief, new understandings and new feelings rush in. Anyone who has ever fallen in love knows how different the world looks when our defensive barriers are lowered. By taking responsibility for awareness, giving up resistance, and forgiveness, we can all begin to take a more active part in lowering our barriers to love and to all the joy that is inside simply waiting to be released.

8

Keeping Love Alive

Mark and Jenny are one of those couples who have everything. She is beautiful and intelligent. He is an attractive, capable man who is rising rapidly in his business. They have a lovely home and two lively, healthy children. Their many friends are admiring and a little envious of the special sparkle that seems to surround them wherever they go. A party is just a bit more fun after Mark and Jenny arrive. Their conversation is wide ranging, and they seem to be interested in everyone and everything.

What their friends do not know is that Mark and Jenny's marriage is in trouble. After six years of sharing the same bed, their sex life has become routine. When they are alone, they have little to say to one another. She has heard all his jokes at least ten times. He has a hard time pretending to be interested in the children's neighborhood adventures or Jenny's club meetings. That special sparkle their friends envy so seems to have deserted them just when all the things they worked to build together are finally materializing.

Mark and Jenny promised one another on their wedding night that their relationship would be different from those dreary alliances they had observed in their youth. They had seen couples sitting together silently in restaurants. They had felt the tension and hostility in their parents' marriages. Not for them, they had vowed. They promised never to go to sleep with a problem unresolved between them, never to treat one another with less than the greatest love and tenderness, never to take one another for granted. Yet all their promises seemed to have come to nothing. Mark and Jenny are considering separation. They hope that some time apart will restore the life to their relationship.

Mark and Jenny are facing an issue that sooner or later confronts all lasting relationships—the difference between their high hopes, their shining expectations and the realities of living together day after day, year after year. At some times even the best relationships will be diminished by boredom, disinterest, mounting interpersonal problems, or destructive fights. Partners may choose to be philosophical about the loss of intensity and interest or to struggle against the growing alienation they feel. It is at times like these that other people may begin to look more and more attractive, that work can begin to command a disproportionate amount of attention and time, that new satisfactions are sought outside the relationship, often contributing to an even greater alienation between partners. Misunderstandings increase and resentments toward one another arise and are left unresolved. Communication breaks down and bitter fighting or silence follows.

What is happening here? Must we settle for less love and involvement with one another than we desire in order to preserve the stability of the relationship? Should we assume that relationships simply wear out in time and that we need to move on in order to find the love that we want in life? What has happened to those beautiful hopes and dreams? Who should we blame: ourselves, our partner, society, the nature of humankind? Perhaps love belongs only to the young, and we must resign ourselves to having outgrown that stage of life. Times like these can raise deep philosophical questions and cause us to re-examine the meaning of our own lives. We may even wonder if there is any purpose to life and if all the things we have valued are not simply fool's gold and empty promises.

In relationships, as in life in general, the presence or lack of a sense of meaning or purpose is dependent on whether or not growth is occurring. Our purpose in life is to grow. We experience a loss of meaning when we allow ourselves to succumb to internally or externally imposed limits to our inherent capacities to learn and to be more than we presently are. The person who leads a life of quiet desperation is the one who has become resigned to being less than what he or she really could be. Whether we resign ourselves or struggle against the limits we face, unless we are in the process of growing, we are in the process of becoming one of the living dead. The world is full of empty faces and empty lives.

Our closest, most personal relationships are delicately balanced and sensitive reflectors of our internal movement toward life or away from it. Tendencies to accept limitations and turn away from growth will invariably result in problems in intimate relationships, often before we are even aware of any difficulty in other parts of life. We can hide from ourselves in work and in social relationships. We can function well and keep our internal problems outside of awareness longer in nearly any activity than we can in our love relationship. The state of our relationship with our most loved and cherished partner is a barometer that predicts the coming highs and lows in the rest of life.

Mark and Jenny and other couples like them have a choice. They can withdraw from one another either by separating or by maintaining the façade of their relationship, or they can admit to themselves and to one another that they have a problem and dedicate themselves to finding a mutually supportive resolution. Eitherway they are probably in for some difficult times, but by choosing to face the situation together they have an opportunity to renew and deepen the love they have shared. Staying together and working things out has the additional advantage of providing a real test of whether or not they have actually grown or simply learned a new way to push the central issues aside. Love flowers and expands between two people who are constantly growing more vital and alive just as it withers under other conditions. It is easy to fool ourselves into believing we are growing when we are simply changing one set of limiting activities for another. It is impossible to fool love.

We all have within us two opposing forces—the urge toward growth and risk taking and the urge toward stasis and stability. Ideally, these forces act together to keep us on a steady track of just enough growth to keep life interesting without introducing so much change at any one time that our coping mechanisms are severely taxed and we are over-whelmed with the stress of handling novel situations. The more we grow, the more we learn that we can handle new situations. When we do this we are able to grow faster and with less conflict and turmoil. The less we grow, the more afraid of growth we become. The result is increasing dissatis-faction with life coupled by ever stronger resistance to change that would restore our happiness and self-confidence. Because we know so little about adult growth and development, it is very difficult for most adults to face up to growth/stability conflicts within themselves. We tend to ignore or talk our-selves out of the thoughts and feelings that are clues to a need for growth. The woman who finds herself chafing at household responsibilities, the man who is growing increas-ingly unhappy in his work, are likely to shrug off their feelings and tell themselves that this is just the way things are until the problem becomes so acute they have to deal with it. People with the strongest will power and the highest sense of respon-sibility are sometimes their own worst enemy in this regard. Ulcers, high blood pressure, and broken relationships are com-mon outcomes of ignoring growth needs.

Current research on adult growth and development indicates that we experience a period of reevaluation at approximately ten year intervals. For many people this evaluation period is inaugurated by a time of emotional upheaval and confusion. Whatever the lifestyle we have constructed for ourselves, it no longer feels appropriate or satisfying. At these times people often consider getting married or divorced, changing careers, having children, or moving to a new location. Making a change may be helpful or necessary in resolving the emotional crisis the individual experiences at these times. However, without an understanding of why we wish to find new structures for our activity, we are just as likely to take a destructive course of action as a constructive one.

A developmental crisis is an invitation to look deeper into ourselves to discover more about the qualities of the essential self that we have not yet recognized and incorporated into our lives. We experience this invitation as a crisis because the forces of stability within have done their job too well. They have blocked growth and risk-taking urges so completely that it takes a painful emotional upheaval to bring our attention back to our need for stability to be balanced by growth. The amount of pain and conflict we feel at such times in life is directly proportionate to how much we have neglected our growth. No one can escape the need for change but we can all develop some understanding of the forces at work within our own personalities that make change both necessary and difficult. When we do so we may be able to avoid the destructive roller-coaster effect that growth/stability conflicts often create.

The major factor that clouds our awareness of the need for growth is our childhood frame of reference carried into adulthood. These old habits of thought, feeling, and behavior may have served us well in childhood, but many of them will limit or prevent our growth as adults until we recognize and transcend them. The good, compliant child who earned love by living up to everyone else's expectations will have to develop some healthy self-assertiveness to be successful in adult relationships. The rebellious child who got attention through resisting other people's demands and insisting on finding his or her own way of doing things, will need to learn cooperative negotiation skills to have a healthy equal partnership with another adult. Everyone has a number of these childhood habits of responding to life. They are so habitual and old that we are usually not aware of them. We plug them into any situation that reminds us of our old relationship with our parents and others and proceed to act them out as if we were programmed like a computer. Parents are noticing this tendency in themselves when they say, "I always vowed that I would never do this to my children, but here I am doing just what my parents did to me. I hated it then and I hate it now, but I can't seem to change."

Childhood programs are much more pervasive than we generally believe. The majority of our behavior and decisions as young adults is in compliance with or in rebellion against the attitudes and patterns of living we learned as children. It is only by experiencing the effect of these patterns in our adult life and learning new ways of handling the situations that confront us that we begin to develop some measure of autonomy. There is no question that we have the ability to act as autonomous, independent people. What we generally do not recognize is that it is not simply a matter of deciding to do so. We need to be able to see the experiences that life brings us as opportunities to expand our awareness of our childhood conditioning and learn new ways of responding that are based on the reality of the present day.

Our intimate relationships help us to do this. Marriage and family life, more than any other adult experience, tend to re-create the patterns and relationships we experienced as children. Since our partner's family was different from our own, we have a chance to observe different ways of responding to old familiar situations. While these different ways may or may not be more effective than our own, at the very least the differences can raise our awareness of the possibility of responding in new ways. For example, a person whose family was invariably polite and restrained in all situations can learn from a spouse whose family responded energetically and emotionally to the smallest happenings. Together, they may be able to evolve new habits of response that take feelings into account while maintaining a sense of perspective and composure.

Intimate relationships bring up a seemingly endless list of old issues for partners to resolve both internally and together.

1. *Issues of power and authority versus compliance and dependency.* When we were very little we had no choice but to comply with the authority of our parents and to depend on their power. We needed their care. An infant cannot survive without it. It can only communicate discomfort and satisfaction and, at best, learn to trust that these communications will be understood and responded to appropriately. As children mature and develop a measure of their own power over the environment, they naturally want to exercise it. "I want to do it myself!" is a phrase familiar to all parents. Every child needs to be allowed the opportunity to do whatever it can for itself. Invariably, however, children will desire to do things they are not yet able to accomplish, and there will be times when parents cannot or will not wait for a child to slowly complete something the parent can do better and quicker. Conversely, there will be things a child will not want to do that it could easily accomplish at that stage of development. Toilet training is one of the best examples of this. Most parents are much more anxious than their children to complete the toilet-training process. Children usually have more interesting things to do than sit on the potty. Psychologists often point to this issue as being the basis for adult problems with authority and control. But toilet training is only one of many similar struggles between parent and child over who will decide how, what, and when things will be done.

I remember a power struggle with my father over shoe

tying. At age six I did not tie my own shoes and did not want to learn. At the time I thought it was because it was too hard, but in looking back I realize I was enjoying the attention I received by still being dependent on my parents to take care of this for me. One day my father refused to tie my shoes and told me to do it myself. I raged and stormed and whined to no avail. Finally, sobbing and feeling very put upon, I retired behind a living-room chair and tied my own shoes for the first time. I felt martyred and resentful for days over my parents' forcing me to do this task that they had always been responsible for in the past.

Power struggles with important figures continue at all levels of development. As adults we are still struggling with those close to us over who, what, and how. Just like children we often want to be totally free to do what we want and never have to be responsible for things that do not interest us. We have learned that these attitudes are immature and unrealistic, so they go underground to pop out again in arguments about how to spend money, who should take out the garbage, and where to go on Saturday night.

The most striking and pervasive of these power struggles is over who will define reality; who is the one who determines what is right and wrong, good and bad in our relationship; who establishes the "shoulds" in our interaction. All of our problems with blame and fault come out of early belief that the person who has the power holds the key to survival. Each partner in a relationship is, at some deep and unconscious level, determined to assume power over their own survival. They see one another as threats to their ability to do this, just as their parents were. Many mundane arguments are symbolic of this deep conflict.

The reality is that as adults we already have or can easily get all the power we need not only to assure survival but to choose the activities that will support us in living a satisfying and productive life. It may be hard work to gain the necessary skills and bring our desires into actuality, but usually we can do much more than we believe we can. We all have a choice just as I did when my father insisted I tie my shoes. I could have refused and fought forever about this, or I could have tied them and then gone to the zoo.

Most power struggles between adults are illusionary conflicts. What we are really looking for is permission to do what we want, because we learned as children that we get into trouble if we act without permission. As adults it is always nice to have the support of those close to us, and there are often real consequences to doing what we want over the opposition of others. This does not mean, however, that others control us. We decide whether what we want is worth risking the consequences, and if we decide it is not, we are often responding to old prohibitions rather than any real constraints in the environment.

One of my clients had decided after several months of treatment for depression to resume the dancing career she had dropped before the birth of her child. She never felt depressed when she was dancing regularly, and she wanted the creative stimulation of working with other dancers. Her husband was totally opposed to this idea and marshalled an army of strong arguments against it—no one could care for their little girl as well as she; she would be absent some evenings when he was home, thus harming their relationship; she would not have the time and energy to do her duties at home; she would not be making much, if any, money and thus it would cost them more than they could afford; he did not like career women, particularly dancers. The arguments went on and on.

My client recognized the child care and household problems her working would raise but had solved them in ways that felt comfortable to her. The money arguments and the implied threats that she would lose her husband's love were more difficult for her to handle. She was scared and enraged over her husband's attitude. For a month they were locked in a classic power struggle which revolved around the issue of the proper role of a wife and mother.

In therapy she saw how familiar this argument was. She had had many similar conflicts with her mother and father while growing up. Both her parents had been very protective of her, their only child, and she had had to struggle for every new freedom gained. It was part of her frame of reference that trying new things caused serious upheavals in her relationships. She recognized that she was communicating her ideas to her husband in such a way as to almost guarantee that he would oppose them. She stopped arguing with him and came up with a new plan. She set up an exercise and dance class with the local YWCA. Part of the fringe benefits of the job was child care in the Y's nursery school. Her salary covered all her expenses, including a weekly cleaning lady. The classes were held in the mornings so that she was always home in the evenings to spend time with her husband. After one week of working, both she and her husband recognized the benefits that their relationship was receiving from the increased energy she was gaining through exercise and the stimulation of interacting with other people. She surprised him with an elaborate birthday gift bought with savings out of her salary. Gradually her contacts in the community led to invitations to dance in various productions and to participate in select dancing classes. Little by little her husband's opposition melted as he saw her determination and felt the benefits of having an energized, exciting, and creative partner. Each time he began to argue with her about what she was doing, she told him she would not argue, but was open to mutually resolving the problem. Their interaction changed from a competitive power struggle to a cooperative problem-solving exchange that had as its basic assumption the conviction that every problem can be solved in a way that benefits all interested parties.

Power struggles can be transcended if we are willing to look at our survival fears, discard those parts of the struggle that are illusionary, and deal with the remaining reality. As in the preceding example, often the resolution results in everyone getting more than they originally hoped for and in a stronger, more exciting relationship.

2. *Issues of responsibility and interdependence versus freedom and autonomy.* As children we do not feel happy if our parents are unhappy with us. At the same time we are unhappy if we cannot have and do what we want. Conflicts between other peoples' needs and our own desires are often unavoidable. Children often learn to believe that their own natural impulses are "bad" simply because they result in punishment or unpleasant consequences like being burned by a hot stove. While many childish impulses are unwise in the sense that they can result in injury or damage to property, they are not, therefore, bad. Being bad implies guilt, the feeling that we have done something we should not have done. Yet how will a child learn about the power of heat and fire without an experience of being burned? No parent would deny the fact that it is better to have a child burn a finger on the stove at age three than to burn down the house at age seven because he or she has never been allowed to find out what fire is all about.

We all have a desire for cooperation and interdependence with another. We are hampered in achieving this state by leftover guilt programs. We believe at a deep level that in order to have a relationship with someone we must always be good. Being good does not always feel good, so we think we must control our impulses, thus limiting our freedom and autonomy in order to be good enough to keep our partner happy with us. Just as we had to be careful not to break mother's vase so she would not be angry, we must take care not to have any impulses that would upset our partner's regard. Relationships, therefore, become a gilded prison. Our desire for harmonious interdependence results in limiting our freedom to grow. Ultimately, no one is happy in this kind of situation.

The conflict between freedom and responsibility is another illusionary issue. Freedom and responsibility are only two aspects of the same thing. One cannot exist without the other. The consequences of acting irresponsibly result in an immediate loss of freedom. The consequences of acting from an attitude of not being free result in actions that are invariably irresponsible and harmful to self and others. For example, a man commits a robbery. Whether he is caught or not, he fears he will be. As a result he must go into hiding and be very careful not to reveal his actions. He can no longer be open about who he is and what he does. He may never go to jail, but he has lost his freedom in an even more basic way.

Another man believes his responsibility to wife and family involves sacrificing his own interests to work at a job he hates. He is exhausted in the evenings and on weekends. He has no time to talk with his wife or to play with his children. He sees no way out of the situation, because he believes his responsibility restricts his freedom of choice. Eventually his wife leaves him, taking the children and charging him with mental cruelty in the divorce action.

When we experience conflicts between freedom and responsibility we can be sure that we are acting out of beliefs that restrict our understanding of the situation. Freedom and responsibility are actually mutually supportive experiences that enhance one another. The freest person is also the most responsible one. The most truly responsible is also the most free. Old childhood rules and beliefs about sin and morality tend to interfere with our ability to perceive this most liberating truth. To find the place where the conflict is transcended we need to allow ourselves to suspend beliefs for a time and look to the messages sent by our essential self. Every time we believe that we are not free we must look at our level of responsibility. Every time we have guilts about not being responsible we need to identify how we have limited our freedom.

Feelings are one pathway to understanding the deeper knowings of our soul. My client, the dancer, discovered that her anger at being blocked by her husband from being free to follow her desires really came out of her own guilt about not being responsible to him, their relationship, and to herself. She realized that her depression was a reflection of having stifled her own creative energy and she recognized that in doing so she was depriving her husband of her love and the stimulation of an energetic life companion. His fear about losing her attention and regard grew out of his own unconscious recognition that she really was not there emotionally anyway. He believed that her physical absence from the home would only make this condition worse. When he found the opposite to be true, not only was he relieved and excited, but he also had the opportunity to learn some new things about his own beliefs concerning freedom and responsibility. My client was able to come up with her remarkably effective plan for resolving the conflict only after she understood her freedom and responsibility conflicts in broader terms. She could have done the same thing out of anger and defiance, smothering her guilt, but it would not have led to such a happy conclusion. As it was she was happy to do the things that would allow her husband to overcome his fears, because she understood that her desire to dance was a life-enhancing impulse of the essential self.

There can be no conflict between real creative impulses and the desire to give and receive love as both are aspects of our essential selves needing to be actualized. One step in any direction enhances our ability to actualize all other parts of our core potentialities. As we grow more free to be our real selves we will naturally be growing in ability to give those closest to us just the kind of love and attention they need to feel truly and deeply satisfied in relationship to us.

3. *Issues of closeness and intimacy versus issues of distance and privacy.* All children are born with a desire to respond and to give love as well as a need to be taken care of and nurtured themselves. If we watch closely we can observe small children attempting to find a way to share and be close. They bring us

the products of their artistic efforts with joy and excitement. Every small achievement is an event to be shared. Every experience is enhanced by having someone to share it with.

I had the opportunity to be present at a child's discovery that blowing puts out small fires. Eighteen-month-old Melissa was shown how to blow out the match that lighted the paper in the fireplace. She was entranced and immediately pointed to a candle across the room making a blowing gesture with her mouth while watching me. Melissa and I were both delighted by the experience, and I have felt very close to her ever since. I felt blessed by the gift of her own excitement that she gave me. Melissa had obviously already learned something about how to get close to people.

Remembering my own feelings when my children were her age, it was clear that Melissa's sharing would not always be so well received. Grownups get tired, have other things on their minds, and are not as endlessly excited and delighted about small miracles as children are. Melissa will have times, as all of us have had, when her sharing will not be received. She will feel hurt and diminished by these experiences. If she has enough of them, she may decide that what she has to offer is not good enough, that her loving energy is not powerful. Many of us made this decision so long ago that we will never remember it. We will still want intimacy and have a strong desire to give love, but we will fear rejection and watch for it to happen. We will look for ways to love others that do not also involve rejection. In the process we can move farther and farther from a true expression of love, because the expression of true love always involves vulnerability.

Children do not have the understanding to recognize that their expressions of love and sharing are not rejected because they are flawed, but because others are not in a position to receive at that moment. As adults we can easily see this if we look, but often our energy is so tied up in defending against rejection that we never see the reality of the situation. Time after time we interpret situations that arise as evidence that our love is not powerful. My dancing client created her depression out of a belief that her love for husband and child was not powerful enough to satisfy them. She was expressing it by cooking, cleaning, and keeping an orderly environment; things that her husband had long since taken for granted. Her original decision to take up dance arose out of an understanding that she was neglecting those parts of herself that were the loving parts so completely that her real loving feelings were obscured. She herself had stopped doing the housework with love and enthusiasm. It had become an empty ritual that she supposed symbolized her love. In fact she was not communicating love to her family, and her family felt it and stopped responding as if she were.

Intimacy is sharing those parts of ourselves that are real and truly exciting to us. It is being willing to reveal real feelings whatever they might be. It is being comfortable with being vulnerable. It is being glad to risk rejection for the joys of the possibilities of closeness.

Another problem that impacts on closeness/distance issues is the belief small children develop about the omnipotence and omniscience of their parents. To a child it sometimes seems that parents are mind readers. Children develop secret lives in order to have some control over their own sense of autonomy. Alert parents often penetrate these secrets, reinforcing a child's belief in parental omniscience. As often as not secrets involve forbidden activities which are then monitored and stopped. The child loses power to act on tabooed impulses and is in fact admonished to control them. Confusion ensues in the child about whose life it is leading—its own or its parents. In adolescence these issues can attain powerful importance. "Don't try to lead my life for me," is one of the battle cries of the teen-age years.

No one would want the contents of their minds reviewed by the general public. We have too many thoughts that we can hardly admit to ourselves and most of us have a number of memories we are not too proud of either. Closeness threatens disclosure. We fear to be unmasked, punished, and worst of all, controlled by another. These feelings bubble up in intimate relationships and give rise to fears of being overwhelmed, consumed, losing ourselves, being dominated, or simply handing over our autonomy and becoming passive slaves to the desires and whims of our partner. The more we tell, the more power they can command over us. We withdraw as much to maintain power as to defend against the hurt of rejection. The very fears we experience are feelings that tell us we are getting close to achieving the experience of unity with our partner that is our heart's desire. We fear it because deep inside we remember that being close to mother sometimes meant she took over. As adults this cannot happen. We do not have to defend our power. It is ours. We cannot get lost in closeness. The nature of intimacy is that it comes and goes like light and dark if we allow it to come at all.

A need for privacy and time just with ourselves is as important a need as the one we have for closeness with others. This is different from withdrawing our willingness to be close. We need time to reflect and contemplate in order to grow and flourish. People who never allow themselves this opportunity will also have trouble being close, because they often will not be in close enough contact with themselves to know what is in their deepest heart. Deeper intimacy with others implies deeper knowing of oneself. There is no real conflict between need for closeness and need for privacy. Again they are just different aspects of the same thing: two complementary ways to gain a greater awareness of ourself and what we have to share with the world.

4. *Issues of commitment and security versus abandonment and risk.* Many adults deeply fear the loss of love. Yet if we look closer at this issue we will see that even more than losing love we fear losing the commitment of our loved ones to staying with us. The dancer's husband eventually recognized that he was willing to overlook his intuitive sense that she did not love

him any more as long as she stayed home and did not actually physically leave him. Many of us would respond similarly.

Most people have a deep fear that they are unlovable. If someone loves us we are surprised and excited. If we believe they have stopped loving us, we feel sad, but usually are willing to live with the situation as long as they stay and do not behave in flagrantly unloving ways. "He/she can have affairs as long as I don't know about it." "He's not home much, but at least he doesn't beat me." "She doesn't like sex, but she's a good mother and meals are always on time."

As children, we felt safe if mother was around. If she left, we felt despair and terror. Young children never know if mother will return and can panic at the sight of her back going out the door. It was not that we necessarily wanted her attention all the time, it was merely that we felt unsafe and afraid if we were prevented from checking in with her when we needed to. Everybody's mother had to leave at some time when we were little. Our society is not set up so that mothers carry their children everywhere. Mothers go to the store and go out to dinner and many mothers go to work. None of us has avoided the terror of childhood abandonment fears. Birth itself was the initial experience of abandonment. Most of us are still dealing with these issues as adults. If we were not we would never settle for the kinds of love relationships many of us have. It is not that most relationships are poor or destructive except in the sense that not achieving the levels of passion and involvement that we are capable of experiencing together is impoverishing and diminishing. The loss of excitement, those feelings of boredom and restlessness, the lessening of desire between us are all clues pointing to the possibility that our abandonment fears have led us to sacrificing passion for security. It is not necessary to do this. We can make a commitment that includes and encourages taking risks with one another. Risks taken successfully build mutual trust and allow for a sense of true safety rather than a stifling security built out of fear. My client, the dancer, took a risk by going ahead with her plans for a job over her husband's opposition. It was a risk taken out of love for herself and for him, and it had almost magical consequences for their relationship. Even if she had taken this risk in anger and defiance, they both probably would have grown. Taking the risk from love assured that mutual trust would be enhanced rather than destroyed, and it saved them from the necessity of continued power struggles over who will make important decisions and where a woman's place really is.

Taking a new look at all of these basic relationship issues is an important first step in breaking out of the constraints and limits we have placed on our experience of love together. Most emotional issues between partners will reflect inner conflicts that relate to at least one of these issues. Big problems usually have components of all of them. Each argument over money, friends, child rearing, sex, chores, or what TV program to watch reflects a difference in frames of reference that arises out of old conflicts with parents, siblings, and other important figures. Every little anger and dispute can open to us an opportunity to see how we can liberate ourselves and our love from the self-constraints we have imposed to insure survival. Keeping love alive, generating passion in life, opening up opportunities for transcendent love to occur, means facing these issues squarely and acting effectively to resolve them. When we do we will not be able to stop feeling excited, powerful, and loving with one another.

9

How to Do It—Together

We are a nation of smart people. We have created a technology unsurpassed any where at any time and we operate within this demanding environment with ease. We hurtle down highways encased in motorized tin cans, we operate complicated machinery and deal with highly sophisticated mathematical concepts every day as we secure our food, clothing, and shelter. All of this we accomplish almost automatically, hardly having to think as we perform complex operations. Given time, money, and the desire, we can solve nearly any technical problem. We have been to the moon, we travel to places on earth that we would never have been able to reach a few short years ago. To our ancestors we would appear as gods.

We spend years in school learning reading, writing, mathematics, and history. Yet when we come together with those we love the most, we are often helpless to solve the most elementary of human problems. Marriages die over issues as insignificant as not having learned how to talk together. Children are alienated from their parents, because we have not learned to come to terms with simple differences in values.

We do not learn to communicate our feelings or to listen to others in school. We are never taught the most elementary rudiments of human dynamics and interpersonal problem solving. If we had ever responded to the long-standing crises in human relationships as we did to the Sputnik scare, we would have achieved by now a human revolution as dramatic as the technological revolution of the latter half of the twentieth century.

As it is we are just beginning to learn a little bit about what it means to be a human being and how to have satisfying relationships with others of our kind. This knowledge has always been available to us but perhaps it is only now when the burdens of mere survival have been lifted and we live long enough and in enough ease to look at ourselves, that we have the energy to attack these problems and find solutions. We are certainly smart enough to do it if we wish.

The opportunities that intimate relationships offer to learn and test new relationship skills make them our school, our testing ground in human development. Since we did not learn many human relation skills in school, our important relationships can provide basic training for developing them in adult life. There are three basic skills everyone can acquire that will clear away the majority of barriers against feeling and expressing love together. They are: straight talk, real listening, and creative problem solving.

STRAIGHT TALK

Honest communication involves responsible sharing of thoughts and feelings. We have all learned communication habits that serve more to confuse than to clarify our meaning. Asking questions like "What would you like to do tonight?" when we mean "I want to spend some time with you," expecting others to read our minds or respond to subtle hints, and blaming others for our feelings ("You make me so mad!") are all examples of unclear communication.

It takes some attention to clear up these habits. The watch word here is "I." Clear statements about thoughts and feelings almost invariably begin with I:

"I want to go to the movies with you."

"I feel scared when you flirt with men at parties."

"I love you."

"I think you are beautiful."

It is profitable to practice making "I" statements. A good exercise is to outlaw any "you" statements for a day or two. If you try it, you may be amazed at how difficult it is to do this. Beware of disguised "you" statements. "I think you are a jerk" is a cleverly camouflaged "you" statement. A straight statement here might be "I'm mad at you" or "I'm really scared about what you are doing."

At a deeper level straight talk means completing your communications with one another. Most of us tend to avoid discussing strong feelings or difficult problems for fear of opening doors we will not be able to go through. There is no way to hide from one another, however. People can tell if another is being honest, is withholding information, or is giving "diplomatic" placating answers. Withholding erodes trust in a relationship. Your partner may not know what is being withheld but will almost always know that something is not quite right. Usually their fantasies about what it might be are worse than the truth. We tend to believe that our worst fears are being realized when there is an ambiguous issue between us. No matter what it is, it is generally better to bring it out in the open. People can handle just about anything if they know what it is they are dealing with. Very few people can manage phantom problems and still feel warm and loving with one another.*

---

* See *How to Love Every Minute of Your Life,* (Hendricks and Leavenworth, Prentice-Hall, 1978), for a fuller discussion of straight talk.

REAL LISTENING

It has become almost tiresomely trite to say that people do not really hear one another's meaning when they listen. Unfortunately, most of us have not heard the message in this yet. Being heard and understood is one of our deepest needs. It is as important as being loved, maybe more so. Everyone feels good when they are really listened to. Real listening implies suspending judgments and criticisms and opening to an awareness of the feelings being communicated as well as the words being said. Since this is so rare, most people will deeply value anyone who can listen well enough to understand them. Millions of dollars are spent each year by people who have hired mental health professionals to do just that. Real listening is very therapeutic. It helps people to know themselves and thus to grow.

It is not too difficult to learn this skill. A way that partners can do this together is to introduce active listening into ordinary conversation. The procedure is for each person to repeat his or her understanding of what the other has said before replying. The first speaker has to agree that the listener's understanding is accurate before going on with the conversation. It may take several tries with the first speaker repeating the original statement and the listener giving back his or her understanding before agreement is reached on what was said. Then the process is reversed with the listener becoming the speaker and replying to the first statement. This also helps sharpen straight-talk skills as one gets instant feedback as to whether or not what he or she has said was understandable. Over time, practicing this technique will help partners arrive at common definitions of terms and a clearer picture of one another's intended meaning in all situations.

CREATIVE PROBLEM SOLVING

Most people do not solve problems very well because they assume that someone must win and someone must lose if there is a conflict of interest. Often problems are not even brought up because of this fear. Ironically this results in both people losing. Creative problem solving begins with the belief that both people can win and that both parties are as dedicated to helping the other party get what they need as they are to seeing that they themselves do. There is no benefit in ducking interpersonal problems if one's goal is to have a loving relationship. Our problems give us a chance to learn more about our relationship and to find more love in one another. Everyone relaxes just a bit when they realize they do not have to defend against being manipulated or taken advantage of. The more we can relax with each other, the more the love between us will flow and grow.

Creative problem solving means looking beneath the surface of the conflict to find out what needs each person is trying to meet. An unreplaced toothpaste cap may mean "I need more space." A late dinner may be a way of communicating a need for more consideration or understanding. When we can get to this level together, problem solving becomes more fruitful. As we expose the real issues between us, petty disputes fall away and we have an opportunity to become more expressive of our love for one another. By acknowledging our own needs we learn to state them more directly and thus enhance our chances of getting them met.

Asking clearly for what you want is absolutely necessary in the creative problem-solving process. Most people are genuinely happy to give the people they love the things they need, but no one can read minds. People first must know what is needed to be able to respond. When asking for what you want, it is most effective to be as clear and specific as possible. For example, if what is needed is a demonstration of affection it is better to say "Please hold me" than "I want you to love me." The other person is more able to respond then, and both of you will know it. Otherwise the response may be "But of course I love you"—very unsatisfactory if what you want is to be held.

BEYOND CREATIVE PROBLEM
SOLVING

Some problems never seem to go away. They come up again and again in different forms. If the toothpaste issue is solved then the conflict will center around the garbage, or the children, or sex. The superficial aspects of the conflict may be different, but underneath the issues at stake seem very similar. You may notice a pattern to your discussions. You know what your partner will say and how you will respond. You can predict what will escalate a discussion into a fight and what the outcome will be. When partners find themselves moving down familiar pathways in their conflicts, pathways they know are ultimately going nowhere, it is a tipoff that a larger issue is at stake. Any difference, even the most petty and insignificant, that sparks strong feelings between partners may symbolize a deeper and older internal conflict in each person.

Since each of us carries within us some unresolved feelings about closeness and distance, risk and stability, power and dependency, and love and abandonment, we are all vulnerable to the revival of old fears. At the same time all of us have an inner urge to resolve these conflicts, as they are barriers to experiencing and expressing our essence. Deep down all of us want to feel comfortable with all our needs— to learn to be close at times and at other times to feel happy being distant; to find the ways to feel free without fear of irresponsibility; to feel safe and loved at the same time we are growing and changing. Intimate relationships can call forth our old conflicts and, at the same time, point to their resolution.

To be able to take advantage of the opportunities offered, it is important to recognize that these problems are inside each one of us. They are personal issues that we are playing out in our relationships so that we can see them clearly and transcend them. Blaming one another only keeps us from growing. What is most effective is to form a mutual alliance to support the relationship and one another in growing beyond these conflicts. Each time we can make a positive step toward resolving these conflicts together, we open the door to transcendent love.

IDENTIFYING THE DEEPER ISSUES

Chuck and Alma came to therapy to find help in deciding whether or not to get a divorce. They had been married only a few years but in that time had nearly lost the ability to enjoy each other's company. Each had many complaints about the other, but they recognized that they had never been particularly bothered before by the things that now caused furious fights. They had lived together for several years before their marriage, so there had really been few unpleasant surprises since then. It seemed they had simply become intolerant of one another, and yet neither was able to break out of the rapidly escalating deterioration of their good feelings for one another.

Chuck's position was that he felt trapped and suffocated. "I just want to get out," he told the therapist. "I don't want to be involved in any relationship that feels as painful as this one. I love Alma, I want her to be happy, but I just can't live with her."

"If you really loved me, you'd stay and work these things out with me. I don't understand why you've become so picky anyway. I seems like you're just looking for an excuse to leave," Alma responded with tears in her voice. "I don't believe you ever loved me. You've just been using me all this time."

Alma went on to say that she felt Chuck had taken advantage of her. "It seems like I give and give and never get anything in return," she cried.

Chuck and Alma were locked in a classic power struggle over closeness and distance needs. Each blamed the other for their problems and each asserted their own individual blamelessness. At the same time, both felt deeply guilty about their conflicts and feared that they themselves were somehow incapable of having an intimate relationship.

The therapist diagrammed their conflict for them:

Closeness = Distance Continuum

Alma $\longleftarrow$ $\longrightarrow$ Chuck
Stay   Go

She pointed out that each one had taken a position on a continuum lying between the two polarities of closeness and distance. It had started when Chuck asserted a need for more time alone at the same time that Alma was pressing for more opportunity for togetherness in their relationship. "She always needed more reassuring than I do," said Chuck. "Part of the reason I married her was to convince her of my love. My job requires a lot of mental effort. I need quiet time just to recharge my batteries. But after we were married she seemed to demand more and more of me."

"As soon as we got married, he just seemed to withdraw more into himself," Alma related. "Before that he used to call me up for lunch and ask me to go away on weekends. Now I hardly see him."

Both Chuck and Alma, once having picked up a role in the closeness-distance conflict, proceeded to behave in ways that pushed each other further along the continuum, until Alma saw herself as a grasping bitch and Chuck hated himself for his cold, unloving attitude toward her. The therapist added to her diagram:

Closeness = Distance Continuum

Alma ←————————————————————→ Chuck
Stay	Go
Grab	Run
Give	Take
Fear	Anger
Suffocation	Alienation
Culturally Female	Culturally Male

She indicated how each of them were responding to cultural stereotyping in the process of choosing sides in a conflict. Women are supposed to be interested in togetherness, feelings, and love, while men should be more independent and strong, not really needing much contact and romance. She suggested that both of them, by picking their own culturally supported role in the conflict, was able to ignore an important part of themselves and, in fact, force the other to act out more and more strongly this neglected piece. Everyone needs both closeness and distance, but neither Chuck nor Alma were aware of the complementary need in themselves that the other was portraying so strongly. She diagrammed this idea:

Closeness = Distance Continuum

The dark side of each whole is the one that we ignore in ourselves.

"Wait a minute!" Alma said as this information sank in. "When I finally just gave up and said 'Okay' to a divorce—

why that's when Chuck suggested we come to see you. Maybe he does really want to be close."

"And I've noticed that Alma has kind of pulled back since we started therapy, just when I've begun to feel better about us," Chuck mused. "Maybe she feels scared of me."

"Yes," responded their therapist. "And you can see how much easier it is for you to be aware of what the other is doing than to see yourself." She finished the diagram of their conflict.

Closeness = Distance Continuum

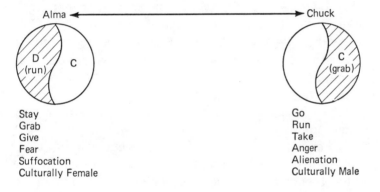

Alma ◄─────────────────────────► Chuck

Stay	Go
Grab	Run
Give	Take
Fear	Anger
Suffocation	Alienation
Culturally Female	Culturally Male

Each partner could see how they were hiding from the little grabber or runner inside that each had forced the other to become. As the reality of this became clear, they both relaxed and began to light up. "You must not be so bad after all," Alma laughed as Chuck reached out and took her hand. Chuck and Alma still had a problem, but at least now they could begin to see what it really was and stop blaming each other for their own discomfort.

Most tenacious long-standing relationship problems arise out of inner conflicts like Chuck's and Alma's. Partners provide one another with a mirror image of the problem, so it is often necessary to look both within and without to learn what one's

own part in it might be. Working together, partners can arrive
at a deeper understanding of themselves and each other by
diagramming their conflicts as the therapist did for Chuck
and Alma. It is important to listen to your partner's description
of your own behavior, and to be as honest and unjudgmental
as possible when talking about each other. The strong feelings
that may arise when you talk are reflections of childhood
feelings and need to be seen as simply more information to
share and diagram. When power issues are being uncovered
it is even more important to stay clear and straight in talking
and in listening. At these times both of you will be especially
vulnerable to feeling manipulated and controlled. The help
of an objective third party may assist you in getting past
rough spots with your good humor intact.

At their next visit the therapist confronted Chuck and
Alma with a choice. "Now that you know what's going on,"
she said, "you have to make a decision. You have established
a pattern together to deal with some inner issues that are
real for each of you. You can continue this pattern, or you
can get a divorce."

"There is another alternative," she went on as both Chuck
and Alma started to protest. "You can work both individually
and together to resolve the inner issues you have been acting
out together. It means hard work, but you may be able to
help one another."

Chuck and Alma had had a wonderful week together.
It had seemed almost like they were seeing each other for
the first time. Their therapist's comments were a little like a
splash of cold water on their excitement. Somewhat sobered,
they began to come to terms with what she had said.

"You mean it's not all fixed?" sighed Alma. "I thought
we were finished with this stuff forever."

"We've had such a good week," Chuck added. "It's been
like when we first met."

After some further discussion the couple realized they
were going to have to do some serious thinking and to work
together closely if they were to prevent a return to their well-

established pattern. Having found their love and delight in one another still alive, they were anxious to give it a try.

DEVELOPING A COOPERATIVE RELATIONSHIP

A cooperative relationship is founded on mutual goals and built out of mutually satisfying processes for achieving those goals. The key words are mutuality and satisfaction. It does not really matter what goals or what kind of processes are arrived at. As long as both partners feel comfortable that the goals they each are to strive for in the relationship are the ones they desire for themselves and one another, as long as other important goals can be met readily outside of the relationship and as long as the process for meeting these goals is workable and equally enhancing to both partners, a cooperative relationship will be assured.

Cooperative relationships cannot be negotiated overnight. The issues of fear of control, competition for frame of reference, power and dependency, etc., all interfere with developing a truly cooperative relationship. What Chuck and Alma discovered about the effect of their inner closeness-distance conflicts on their ability to be together comfortably is true for all of us. These issues need to be resolved both internally and interpersonally before a true cooperative relationship can evolve. However, any couple can begin to build one at any time. All it takes to start is a willingness to work together for growth. Even the process of doing the groundwork will be growthful.

DEVELOPING THE CONTRACT

It is a good idea to put your agreements about goals and processes down on paper. Both partners need to write down their own hopes and dreams for the relationship. It is best to start out by being just as idealistic as you can. Later you can get more realistic if necessary. Come together to share your list sometime when you will not be disturbed and begin comparing your goals. If some goals seem mutually exclusive, note them for later work. In this first meeting simply identify the common goals and spend some time sharing fantasies of how your relationship would be and how you would feel if you could meet these goals. Then begin identifying the barriers you see. What are the things that are stopping you from feeling the way you want to feel together right now.

Here are some things from Chuck and Alma's list:

ALMA
Dynamic, passionate, intimate relationship with Chuck on a day to day basis

Plenty of money to buy people things, me included, and to travel, etc.

Enough free time to enjoy cooking, gardening, making a quilt, and other ordinary tasks

Meaningful work that excites me and where I can make a contribution

Children

Beautiful, comfortable, orderly and serene surroundings

CHUCK
Always feel fulfilled

Comfortable yet dynamic environment to stimulate creative ideas and work

Relaxed, slow and langorous relationship simultaneously charged with happy intensity

To be totally supported and understood by Alma in all that I do

Easy free flow of communication—no hassles, no arguments

Opportunity for travel and adventure; no barriers to becoming all that I can be and succeeding in my career

Sharing their lists was exciting for Chuck and Alma and at the same time somewhat frightening. There was commonality in their lists and some implicit problems. Chuck didn't mention children, an important goal for Alma and one that seemed impossible for her to fulfill outside of the relationship. Alma also noticed a stress on work, no arguments and her support of Chuck in his list and was worried that she would lose out on the closeness she wanted from him. Chuck wondered how Alma was going to have money, travel, free time and children as well as work, and was afraid he might be trapped into supporting her and a bunch of kids, thereby limiting his freedom to risk and grow in his work. Striving for the kind of success Chuck wanted was chancey and might lead anywhere. He did not want fear for his dependents to get in the way. When pressed by Alma he was ready to say he did not want dependents at all.

The next step is for each individual to make a list of the barriers identified by both partners and generate a list of twenty or thirty positive solutions to each barrier. This may take some thinking. Each solution you add should take into account both partners' needs and feel good (not necessarily marvelous) to you. This can be done, although it seems a formidable task at first. If you get stuck, ask friends for ideas, but be sure to write down only those that are acceptable to you. This task will probably take at least a week. Do not take longer than two weeks to complete it and have your next meeting.

In some cases old resentments between partners will be barriers to trust and commitment. As these come up they can be handled in a special way. Even if they do not come up at first, it is helpful to the process to take time out at this point and to list every grievance you have against one another no matter how petty or how large and painful. Once you complete the list, working alone and again in writing, forgive your partner for every grievance. Keep working on this until you actually feel the forgiveness. Grievance lists are for forgiveness, not to be shared.

Alma worked for days on forgiveness. Her list of grievances got pretty long but she was determined to give it a try for her own sake as well as Chuck's. Here are a few excerpts from her diary. The process took about a week:

> "I forgive Chuck for all my grievances. (It's hard to forgive without wanting a return. Is that forgiveness? I want him to change. I can't stand it if he keeps this stuff up.)
>
> "I forgive Chuck for all my grievances. (If I forgive him he'll just go on hurting me. I want to be able to defend myself. I've run out of tolerance for criticism and unpleasant surprises. Resentment is in my bones.)
>
> "I forgive Chuck for all my grievances. (It seems pitiful to have spent all this time hurting each other. I feel sad. Maybe I don't see him accurately. I'm sure he is a good person but why does he keep hurting me?)
>
> "I forgive Chuck for all my grievances. (Why not forgive him? After all I could have left him many times but I didn't. Besides—I've learned a lot from all this . . . but if I forgive him he'll do it all again.)
>
> "I forgive Chuck for all my grievances. (We have a clean slate now and can move on, free of the past. If I don't forgive him, we can't go anywhere.)
>
> "I forgive Chuck for all my grievances. (?)
>
> "I forgive myself for allowing myself to be undervalued."

Alma went on in this manner until the only response that came into her mind was "Yes, of course I forgive him and myself too." She still goes back to this process when she feels unsatisfied or notices herself having angry thoughts about the past. "Forgiveness is probably a lifelong process," she told her therapist. "At least it is for me. But I like it. I feel freer and happier now than I have in years. I think I'll forgive a few more people while I'm at it."

The third step in developing a cooperative relationship

is to bring together your barrier lists—which you may have added to—and your solutions for sharing and discussion. Talk over your feelings and the advantages and disadvantages of the solutions suggested. Keep your minds open to more ideas: you may have several good ones. Make note of them. Do not make any decisions at this time. Just remain open to your feelings and to the possibility that you both can get everything you want.

At your next meeting you will be ready to make some decisions. Some of your goals may have changed by now, others may be strengthened and more clearly defined. Reach agreement on as many goals as you can and begin discussing how other goals could be met in other ways. Chuck realized that he could get understanding and support from many people at those times when Alma could not meet these needs, without threatening their relationship. Together Chuck and Alma decided to develop an emergency fund over the next two years so that Chuck would feel safe about taking risks in his business. Alma also decided to try some free-lance work herself, just to see if she would be able to work on her own and have more control over her time. Chuck agreed to back her in this, since he found that the idea of having a child became more interesting to him the more he thought about it. Alma felt closer to Chuck and not so scared that he would run off or ignore her.

Those goals that remained unresolved required another round of thinking. More inner work on the conflicts will generally illuminate underlying issues and ultimately result in new, related goals emerging. Other unresolved goals just need another appraisal and more alternatives developed and discussed. As long as both partners remain firm in the desire to meet their own and one another's needs freely, continuing to negotiate will ultimately be rewarding. A good therapist or an understanding and skilled friend can be of inestimable value here.

The final step before writing your contract is to determine a problem-solving process that will work and feel good to both partners. Some partners may decide to lock themselves in a room until agreement is reached. Others may want to take a break and think things through alone. One couple I know discusses touchy areas while making love. This helps them to stay in tune with one another's feelings and to reassure each other of their love. Many people would find this disasterous, but it works for this couple. Some people write notes to one another. My husband and I often work out problems in a restaurant or some other public place. This helps us to keep our cool or at least hold our tongues when to speak would be unwise. The aura of the business lunch provides a straightforward context for discussion of thoughts and ideas, and most issues are cleared up with dispatch. If feelings run too high, we simply postpone the discussion until another day.

Most partners will probably not be able to avoid all fights. It is important to distinguish between problem solving and fighting, however. If we are fighting it is because we have some strong feelings to share. Sharing angry feelings is just as important as sharing loving ones. But strong feelings also get in the way of the kind of clear thinking that is necessary for creative problem solving. Trying to solve problems in anger does not work well. It can create power struggles which intensify anger and fear, usually unnecessarily. When you have strong feelings to share you can do it using "I" statements and set aside another time to define the problem and find creative solutions that will work for both partners. We can learn to accept one another's feelings gracefully and without fear when we know that our problem-solving procedures will result in positive solutions and mutual growth.

Once your contract is complete, type it up and have a notary witness your signatures. This lends the seriousness of a legal document to your agreement. Since people's needs change, relationships must change too. A relationship contract is never finalized. It needs to be organic—growing and changing. Regular review times and re-negotiation procedures need to be built into the contract itself. If your relationship is to last a lifetime it must be able to develop and change to reflect the inevitable change of the partners.

ADULT DEVELOPMENT CAN CREATE RELATIONSHIP PROBLEMS

The crisis periods in adult development can put serious strain on relationships. The person who is in developmental crisis experiences discomfort in all areas of life—the more emotional involvement, the more intense the discomfort. Relationships that seemed just fine can suddenly feel emotionally constricting. The partnership is still operating under the old agreements which will probably eventually need re-evaluation and some change. Meanwhile the spouse in crisis does not know what he or she wants. Adults in crisis only know that things need to be different. This leads to confusion and conflict in the relationship. It is upsetting to a spouse who has been operating in good faith to find out suddenly that everything they are doing is wrong. At the same time it is important to have some compassion for the partner who is experiencing developmental crisis. No one can avoid them entirely. Everyone needs understanding at these times and also some help working things through. It is a good idea for the person in crisis to be aware of the possibilities of alienating those close to them, those who are potentially their greatest helpers.

Additionally, developmental crisis invariably brings up old conflicts of the sort described in the last chapter. The crisis itself is really about finding new ways of resolving these conflicts in order to release previously undeveloped parts of the essential self. One's spouse often has to bear the brunt of the unacknowledged side of these conflicts. As we saw in the case of Chuck and Alma, we can actually force one another to play the part in our conflicts that we are not willing to look at.

Many divorces come out of situations like this, but divorce does not resolve the issue. The conflict is inside—and try as we might, we can never get a divorce from ourselves. As soon as the stress of the immediate situation is alleviated, our needs on the other side of the conflict will re-emerge, and we will re-create the same situation. If Chuck were to leave Alma, he would probably soon fall in love with another woman. When eventually they married, the same problems would emerge. His other alternative, to stay distant and aloof from intimacy will never be particularly satisfying to him. Sooner or later he will find himself locked in the same problems again and again until he confronts and resolves the inner issues.

A developmental crisis is painful for both partners. People who love one another worry over each other's depression and frustration. Relationships usually are not as much fun when one partner is in crisis. Yet these are the times when constancy and intelligent management of the crisis can lead to a dramatic renewal of transcendent love. Using the techniques of uncovering and integrating feelings, and of forgiveness along with some systematic analysis of the deeper inner issues, will help separate the realities of the present day relationship from old beliefs stemming from childhood.

How to Love Every Minute of Your Life (Hendricks and Leavenworth, Prentice-Hall, 1978), and *Transformations* (Roger Gould, Simon and Schuster, 1979), are two books that have helpful information on resolving the archaic issues in a developmental crisis. It can be extremely effective to work with a psychotherapist during a developmental crisis, especially if intimate relationships are under stress. This takes some strain off the partner and shortens the period of internal distress as well. Crisis periods are rich growth opportunities. A well-managed developmental crisis will lead to a fuller and more satisfying experience of life and can be a prelude to the revitalization of passionate love.

Love is like a circle that completes life. We all need one

another, not in a neurotic, dependent way but in a healthy, expanding way. We each need someone for loving and sharing, to teach us more about ourselves and to join with us in an experience of ever-deepening intimacy and the endless variations of passionate love. Developing real loving relationships is one of life's greatest challenges and the reward of meeting this challenge is having your heart's desire.

10
Expanding Opportunities for Transcendent Love

We do not have to wait for relationship problems or a developmental crisis to have more transcendent love in daily life. Those wonderful feelings of love are always inside us. Sometimes it is simply the press of business or the routine of daily living that distracts us or deadens our awareness of our loving self.

Many people believe that a love relationship will automatically fulfill them. Once the courtship period has passed and the relationship becomes comfortable, they turn their energy into other areas of life. This can lead to stagnation in the relationship. Love is like a garden. Once the seeds of love have been planted they still need tending and care if they are to grow and flourish, just as a garden needs to be watered and cultivated if it is to bear fruit and flowers. Lovers need time together to harvest the fruits of their love. The more love we share with one another, the more love will grow between us, just as the more we pick our tomatoes and beans, the more vegetables the plants produce.

In this chapter and the next we will explore a variety of ways to enhance closeness and intimacy, thereby opening more doors to the experience of transcendent love. Some of these experiences will appeal to you and others may not. Some will be more appropriate at some times than at others. Once you get started in experiencing new ways of being together, you will think of more that are uniquely suited to you, your partner, and your relationship. Be adventurous in trying new experiences together. Even if you are uncomfortable at first, you may learn to love it!

Transcendent love cannot be hunted down and captured. It can be invited into our lives gently, with humor and love. Any experience or activity that takes us deeper into our true essence as human beings is a pathway to transcendent love. Partners who can learn to share a part of the path with one another will reap the benefits of an ongoing renewal of their love for one another.

QUALITIES OF A LOVING RELATIONSHIP

Every relationship has its own unique configuration of characteristics, yet there are a number of qualities that are common to all positive love relationships. These form the basis upon which a lifetime of loving can be built. Your relationship may exhibit some or all of these qualities. There may be some that you want to develop more strongly. If so, you can do it together and, in the process, strengthen your loving bond.

No person or relationship is automatically perfect. All the basic qualities of expressing love and building a loving relationship can be learned. Practicing the expression of these qualities enhances the individual partners and the relationship, just as aerobic exercise strengthens the cardiovascular system. There is nothing wrong with feeling awkward and uncomfortable about expressing your love. Most of us feel that way at least part of the time. If you start to do it anyway, you will find yourself feeling more comfortable and spontaneous as time goes by. The more you practice, the easier it will become, until you find your loving feelings flowing smoothly and easily and you experience the benefits of increased energy and creativity that go hand in hand with the ability to express the loving part of yourself freely and without fear.

Caring.   Caring implies a sincere emotional bond between people. When we care for people, we are naturally interested in them and in their well-being and happiness. We want to know what they are thinking, feeling, and doing. We want to respond to them in ways that will enhance their lives. We feel concern when they are ill or emotionally upset. We feel good about their successes.

Caring does not mean, however, that our own feelings are tied to or dependent on another's. If a loved one is unhappy, we do not need to be unhappy as well to express our caring. Simply being there, listening and offering comfort is often all that is needed. Caring also sometimes means saying "no" or confronting people if their behavior does not seem to be serving their own best interests.

For example, Mark and Abby were both very excited when they learned that Mark had received a big promotion. They knew that Mark would be working very hard at first to learn his new job and this would mean they would have less time together for awhile. Abby was not worried about this because she knew the situation would only be temporary. She did begin to worry when, as the time grew closer for Mark to take over his new job, he was suddenly beset by a series of minor physical ailments and small irritating accidents. Abby knew Mark was under some stress and did not want to add to his problems. But, the more she thought about it, the more she suspected that Mark was keeping some of his own apprehensions about his new job to himself.

"He has never been accident prone before," Abby thought. "This is all just too much of a coincidence." Both Mark and Abby knew that suppressed feelings can sometimes express themselves through illness or accidents. Abby decided to confront Mark with her hunch that he was trying to ignore some of his feelings. That evening they had a long talk about Mark's fears and hesitancies about his new job and how much he missed spending time at home. Mark decided to pay more attention to these feelings in the future, and as he did, his physical problems cleared up. If Abby had chosen not to worry Mark with her concerns both of them probably would have become even more uncomfortable about Mark's new job and the unexpressed feelings in their relationship. As it was, she was able to express her caring for him despite her hesitancies, and both of them benefited.

Trust.   Trust grows out of honesty and taking responsibility for keeping agreements in a relationship. Knowing you can depend on your partner to tell you the truth, to be on time, to remember an errand, or to let you know if it is impossible to keep a promise is very reassuring. The deepest trust we can develop with one another, however, goes beyond simply being reliable and avoiding deception. It arises out of an active commitment to nurturing and tending the relationship. It is the result of a deep conviction that whatever happens, both partners are willing to work together to achieve maximum benefit for one another and for the relationship.

Being trustworthy does not mean being self-sacrificing. It does mean being clear with each other about your wants, needs, desires, feelings, and thoughts. If you know you can depend on your partner to tell you when he or she is angry, you need never worry or wonder about how to interpret a mood or a silence between you. If you know you can always approach your partner with your own feelings, you will be freer to be the spontaneous you that adds sparkle to your relationship. Trust is the foundation of any partnership. It is a fragile condition, easily ruptured, and needs consistent active attention to deepen and grow.

Giving.   A warm "hello," a gentle touch as you pass one another in a crowded room, a phone call in the middle of a busy day, a simple "I love you"—all of these are small but important gifts we can give to the person we love. This kind of giving means far more to a relationship than gold watches at Christmas or birthday diamonds. Giving means taking the time to share the positive thoughts and feelings we have about one another. "You look beautiful," "I admire the way you handled that problem with the kids," "You take my breath away when you look at me like that"—all these expressions of positive experiences we have together often remain unspoken. Each time we do express them we add to the love magic between us.

Everyone needs loving recognition and an acknowledgment of their importance to others who are important to them. Many people become stubborn about this and refuse to give of themselves because they believe they will not be given to in return. One of my clients expressed a typical problem that many couples have with giving. "I've asked George again and again to be more demonstrative and affectionate. I've even told him specifically what I want—a kiss when he comes home, a hug sometime during the day. Well, he does these things for a while, but they seem forced and wooden. Then he stops. Sometimes I wonder if he really loves me or even *sees* me."

A loss of warmth and expressiveness in a relationship erodes trust and loving feelings. My client was feeling less and less interested in her sexual relationship with her husband and was beginning to be bored with their evenings and weekends together. She solved her problem by telling George how she felt about the lack of warmth between them, and then putting her energy into giving him the kinds of things she wanted for herself. At first this was difficult for her to do. "I'm afraid I'm going to be taken advantage of. I feel angry at him, not loving at all," she said. Once she examined her feelings carefully, however, she realized that although many of them were angry ones, she also had positive feelings about George every day. She made an effort to express them whenever they came up and were real for her. If he were not actually with her at the time, she might write a note to leave on his pillow or arrange some flowers for his desk. When he came home, *she* hugged and kissed him warmly. "I found out one thing," she told me later. "A hug feels good no matter who starts it. I like hugging him as much as I like him hugging me." George was delighted by all this attention. Soon he was calling home almost every day, stopping occasionally to pick up a special wine, and even leaving his own notes for her. Their relationship bloomed. Soon they were able to have a constructive discussion about their mutual needs for warmth, and they established a firm commitment to giving to one another. This commitment is still growing and blossoming. They have become very creative in thinking of new ways to surprise one another with their love. Just recently George arranged a special outing for them starting with breakfast in bed and ending with a romantic candlelight dinner. "I think it was the best day in my life," my client told me. "That man must really love me!"

Acceptance. Acceptance does not mean always agreeing with your partner and never disliking something he or she might do or say. It does mean being willing to listen uncritically and unjudgmentally to another's thoughts, feelings, and point of view. Acceptance implies an attempt to understand how your loved one sees things—what meaning he or she gives to life and the events of life. Acceptance sometimes means recognizing and learning how to handle differences in values and priorities that may initially appear to be in direct conflict.

The key to acceptance is within yourself. As we move though life we all find that some of the things we encounter are easy to accept and others very difficult. Usually, the things we find easiest to accept are the familiar things; the qualities and values others hold are more acceptable, the closer they are to our own. Differences among people, however, are very real. They are what makes life rich, fascinating, and full of abundant possibility. Partners who can learn ways of accepting one anothers' differences and working with them in positive ways grow in flexibility, understanding, and love.

Resignation is not acceptance. Learning to be more accepting of one another is an active process involving developing an awareness of how our differences affect our feelings about ourselves and each other, sharing those feelings, and working together to enhance the positive aspects of these differences, rather than dwelling on the negative. When people begin to look at the differences between themselves and their mate, they often find that many of the troublesome ones are also a source of joy and strength in the relationship.

One couple I know were deeply in love but uncertain whether to marry because of some rather extreme differences over the values of order and stability in the home. His apartment was always a mess, his clothes in disorder, his plans constantly changing. He tended to move his residence often, usually about once a year. He started many projects, finishing a few, and leaving many half complete. She, on the other hand, was quite orderly and felt uncomfortable when projects did not quickly move forward toward completion. It was difficult for her to put work down and shift into another activity before finishing a task. He felt that she was rigid and compulsive in her habits. She worried that he would be an unreliable partner and create more confusion in her already active and demanding life. Despite this she admired his sense of fun and spontaneity. When he did persuade her to disrupt her schedule for a walk, a movie, or a weekend trip to Mexico, she always had a wonderful time. Conversely, he admired her organizational skills, her ability to solve complicated logistical problems, and the serenity that seemed to surround her wherever she went.

Once this couple started analyzing their differences and admitting to one another the fears and irritations that each felt about them, they began to see some positive ways to enhance the benefits and diminish the likelihood that their differences would create serious relationship problems. They learned that it was not that he enjoyed disorder in his environment, but that his mind was constantly generating so many creative ideas that he simply could not be bothered with stopping to clean up after himself. He could barely keep up with his mental energy as it was. Since his creativity was a large part of his attractiveness for her, she found she had no desire to put any barriers in its way. They eventually decided to employ her organizational strengths to figure out how he could continue his own pattern of working without infringing on her sense of comfort. They decided to buy a house together that provided a space that was solely his to be as messy in as he needed to be. They figured out what a reasonable equal division of household responsibility involved and then she hired people to do his share and some of her own. She became more tolerant of upsets in her daily routine and more able to respond to spontaneous invitations the more she was able to see that there were solutions to the problems she feared and that she wanted and needed his sense of fun and creativity to spark her own. He appreciated having an orderly space to come into when his work was finished and often consulted with her on ways that he could complete his projects more efficiently. Both of them ultimately felt energized and excited by their differences far more often than otherwise. They each felt better about themselves too. He began to perceive himself as a responsible person rather than the unreliable sort he had secretly feared he was. She felt freer, more open, and more able to have fun and enjoy herself.

Acceptance of differences can lead to many self- and relationship-enhancing experiences. Listening to one another, openly acknowledging the various feelings we have about our differences without criticism or judgment, and looking for the strengths we perceive in our differences can take us a long way toward learning to love in one another many things we may have initially feared.

Empathy.   Empathy is the ability to "feel with" another person. It means being able to put yourself in another's place and understand the feelings behind what they are thinking and doing. Everyone experiences the same basic feelings of anger, fear, sadness, joy, and excitement. All of our other feelings are forms or combinations of these basic five. Irritation is mild anger. Jealousy is a combination of anger, fear of loss, and perhaps some sadness. Anxiety is a form of fear. If you know how you feel when you are excited or angry, then you can be fairly confident that you can understand how other people feel when they say they are experiencing one of those feelings.

The problem with empathy is that people differ in how they show and express their feelings. For example, one person who is feeling fear may withdraw emotionally or run away, while another in the same situation might express the feeling by blaming or criticizing others. A third might deny feeling afraid at all and outwardly appear to be cool and confident. In order to develop empathy with our loved ones it is important to learn how they tend to behave, what they say and do, when they are experiencing various feelings.

Empathy is both developed and expressed by listening openly and nonjudgmentally and by gently encouraging another to share his or her feelings. Some feelings are easy to see and understand. A happy grin speaks for itself. Others are more subtle and illusive. Silence can imply many things ranging from peaceful contentment to boiling anger. If someone seems upset or depressed to you, you can express empathy by simply saying, "You seem upset. Would you like to talk about it?"

Empathy is important in loving relationships. It is one way to express caring and the desire to understand and support one another through the good times and the bad times. Everyone has a deep need to be understood. Being able to share feelings without fear of criticism builds confidence, trust, and intimacy in loving relationships.

Sharing. Joint activities, making a home together, socializing with friends—these are all ways that partners in a relationship can share themselves with one another. The most important kind of sharing, however, is sharing yourself. A relationship deepens and grows when both partners are willing to invest energy and thought in keeping one another up to date on what is happening inside themselves and in their lives apart from one another. Talking about a problem at work, relating the joy you felt on an early morning run, or giggling together over a child's antics brings partners closer in friendship and in love.

To be able to share with another means being willing to become vulnerable with that person. All of us have feelings and thoughts that we do not like. Most of us hide many insecurities, fears, and embarrassments behind our social masks. Taking off those masks with one another is difficult at first, but ultimately it is relieving and freeing. If someone loves you with your mask off, you know that it is really *you* that is loved. The interesting thing about being open and vulnerable is that people actually tend to like you better that way than with your mask on. The reality of you is always more exciting than any part you can play.

Partners in a relationship both need to take responsibility for sharing. Many relationships are unbalanced in this regard with one person constantly initiating or asking for sharing and the other resisting the process. Pay attention to your own level of sharing. Do you feel that you do too much, too little, or is there a good balance in your relationship? Are there subjects that you avoid talking over or things that you tend to withhold from your partner because you are afraid of creating conflict? Withholding a part of yourself from a loved one always creates a barrier to the experience of transcendent love together. At our deepest level we all want to be known by and to truly know the people we love. Being vulnerable with those we love and depend upon can feel very risky at times. But it is only by taking risks in our relationship that we can open the door to the excitement and intimacy of real loving exchange.

CHECKING YOUR RELATIONSHIP

The development of the qualities of caring, trust, giving, acceptance, empathy, and sharing tends to dissolve many relationship problems and cause others to become less stressful and more easily managed. When partners experience these qualities in their relationship, an environment of good will is created that sustains them both in periods of stress. The happy times become more joyful too, initiating an upward spiral of closeness and growth.

There is no relationship in which these qualities are all perfectly developed. You may be strong in empathy but less expressive of caring and your partner will have strengths and weaknesses in other areas. This can be very positive, because it means that you and your partner have some interesting and exciting tasks ahead if you wish to invest yourselves in the task of enhancing some of these qualities in your daily life together.

The first step is to check out how you both feel about the level of expressing these qualities that exists in your relationship now. You can do this quickly by taking the short test that follows. Each of you can rate yourself on your expression of each one of the qualities and then rate your partner in how you perceive their expression.

QUALITY	LOW				HIGH
Caring	1	2	3	4	5
Trust	1	2	3	4	5
Giving	1	2	3	4	5
Acceptance	1	2	3	4	5
Empathy	1	2	3	4	5
Sharing	1	2	3	4	5

When you compare your answers you may find some surprising differences. You may find you have rated yourself high on a quality that your partner perceives you low in expressing. For example, this may indicate that while you are feeling very caring toward your partner, the ways in which you express your caring are not getting through. Perhaps your partner is just not noticing what you are doing. On the other hand you may have different definitions of what caring means or different ideas about caring behavior. You can discuss any differences you find in an uncritical, nonblaming way. When your intent is to discover ways to enhance your relationship, there is no reason to feel bad if you find one. Every difference you discover, every underdeveloped quality you find, only indicates that there are ways you can increase your enjoyment of one another.

INCREASING THE EXPRESSION OF LOVING QUALITIES IN YOUR RELATIONSHIP

Once you are clear about how you and your partner perceive the level of expression of the various loving qualities in your relationship, you can take the next step. With some of the qualities, you will find that your expression is very satisfying to both of you. In that case you can simply keep on doing what you are doing and focus your attention in areas where you and your partner want to grow. The exercises and experiences that follow will help you focus on particular areas. As you define more clearly what you need from one another and what each of you is willing to give, you will begin to reap the benefits that real sharing brings to a relationship.

The key to this process is mutuality. Both of you need to feel comfortable with all the solutions you agree to implement. You do not need to feel that you can do them perfectly or even well, but it is important to be clear with yourself and each other that you want to learn and are willing to invest some of your time, thought, and energy into doing so. With this intention clearly in mind you will begin a process that is not only relationship-enhancing, but self-enhancing as well.

Increasing the Expression of Caring. The things that feel caring to you may not be the same things that help your partner to feel cared for. Most often we tend to give the things that we want in return. This exercise will help you both uncover new ways to show your caring for one another. Begin by setting up an appointment to discuss caring in your relationship. Before the appointed time each of you should list all the things you can think of that mean feeling cared for by another person. Give specific examples, that is, "Showing concern for my well-being by asking me how my day went and by helping me think about problems at work." Place a star by each item on your list that you think your partner already does. Then make another list of the things that you do to show caring for your partner. Bring these lists to your meeting.

When you meet together, exchange lists and spend some time silently thinking over what the other person has written. You may find that you are having some unpleasant feelings—anger, guilt, feeling unappreciated, are a few that some people experience at this point. Go ahead and experience those feelings, continuing your silence until both of you are feeling centered again and able to listen to one another. At this point you can ask one another for clarification of any points you do not understand or for more specific examples for the various items on your lists. Keep in mind that you are trying to understand your differences, not to justify yourself or find a culprit. There is no right or wrong way of expressing caring, only ways that work in your own relationship and ways that do not. If you have been feeling self-sacrificing about doing something for your partner that is not included on his or her list, then it is important to take responsibility for your feelings about this rather than to blame your partner for being insensitive. Some couples like to meditate together during this second period of silence. If you would like to try this there are some meditations to choose from in the next chapter.

When you are ready to go on to the next step, mark the things on your partner's list that you are willing to start doing and to continue to do to express caring in your relationship. Take turns telling one another what you will do. Then write a contract that includes all of the things each one of you has offered to do and a commitment to doing at least one of these things each day. Be sure to include things that take little energy like saying "I love you" with warmth and feeling, as well as things that might take more energy or time, like serving breakfast in bed. Each of you sign the contract and keep a copy for yourself.

In the days ahead avoid judging one another's performance, but do be generous to one another in acknowledging caring gestures. If a hug feels good, say so. If you appreciated a phone call, let your partner know that. Beginning to express more caring has a cumulative effect. The more you do, the better you feel, and the more you want to express. Talking over your good feelings with one another speeds up the process.

Another way to enhance caring in your relationship is to take turns arranging a day or an evening once a week just to show the other how much you care. You might want to take your partner out or to stay home with candles and soft music. Whatever you decide to do for your partner, the important thing is that you are there to do nothing but show them in ways that work how much you care. Some couples enjoy massage or hours of uninterrupted sex or talking quietly together over a good meal and a bottle of wine. Others enjoy dancing or sharing a special play or concert. You and your partner may enjoy all of these things. There is no limit to the varieties of ways we can show the people we love how much we love them. Just let your creative imagination flow. Brainstorm or fantasize together about what the perfect evening or day would be for each of you. Develop as many ideas as you can from these sessions, try new things together, let the secret romantic in you come out.

Building Trust.   Stand three to four feet apart, but rather than facing each other, face in the same direction. Whichever partner is in front allows him or herself to fall backward without attempting to break the fall in any way. The partner behind catches the falling partner under the shoulders to break the fall and lowers him or her gently to the floor.

This is an exercise that builds trust. The person who falls back has no way of telling whether he or she will be caught until it actually happens. Try it together. If you are worried about falling or dropping your partner, try it first with a mattress or pillows on the floor. Very small people can catch even very large people this way and lower them to the floor without injury to either. People with back problems should avoid this exercise.

We build trust together in many very subtle ways. Acting in honest and trustworthy ways toward one another is of course the basis for building trust together. Other experiences can expand that trust. The trust fall described above is one excellent way. Sharing other physical activities that require cooperation and teamwork for success enhances our trusting connection. Rock climbing or playing tennis doubles together are two of many joint physical activities that can strengthen trust at an important nonverbal level.

Sometimes trust is eroded in a relationship because partners do not clearly understand what they expect from one another. Some expectations that we have also may be unreasonable or impossible for the other to fulfill. If we keep our expectations a secret from one another then we are always in danger of failure or disappointment. You can get your expectations out into the open by trying the next exercise.

Place two straight chairs about three feet apart facing one another. Sit erect with legs uncrossed and hands relaxed in your laps. Maintain eye contact. Breathe deeply two or three times. Then each take a turn completing the following sentence:

I trust you when _____.

Again breathe deeply, continuing to maintain eye contact, and then take turns completing the following sentence:

I don't trust you when _____.

Repeat this experience three or four times and then stand, clasp hands, and close your eyes. Breathe deeply, allowing yourself to feel any feelings that you are experiencing. Now open your heart and allow yourself to feel your love flowing out to your partner and back again from your partner to you.

Do this exercise as many times as necessary to get out all of your expectations of one another. It may take you a few weeks to complete this process. Again in your statements of trust and mistrust be as specific and as nonjudgmental as you can be about the behavior of your partner. Your purpose here is to share something important about yourself, not to criticize the other.

Just being able to share your trustful and mistrustful feelings with your partner will result in a greater feeling of trust between you. As you work through these feelings you may uncover some problem areas. Some of your own or your partner's expectations may not be realistic. Others you or your partner may not wish to meet. You may be able to find new ways to handle these situations so that trust can still be maintained. If your partner expects you always to be on time and you are sometimes unavoidably detained, perhaps a phone call whenever possible would keep the trust level high and develop a trust reserve that will stretch to cover those times when it is impossible to call. If there are some expectations that simply cannot be met and no alternative solution can be found, at least you will both know that and acknowledge this factor in your relationship. When this happens, the issue may still be a problem but is no longer necessarily a test of trust in the relationship.

Developing the Quality of Giving. Increasing the level of giving in a relationship helps people to see one another with fresh eyes. There are so many things to appreciate in one another, but just as we forget to stop and smell the roses in our rush to get through the day's business, we often do not take time to experience and express our mutual appreciation.

Find a comfortable place to sit together where you can touch your partner's hand and look into each others' eyes. Take turns telling each other five things you appreciate. Notice your own reactions to your partner's appreciations. Do you feel embarrassed? Happy? Scared? Share your feelings about being appreciated and expressing your appreciations with one another. Then repeat the whole experience with five new appreciations. Do not judge your feelings. Just let them flow. If you enjoy meditating together, do a short meditation after the second round of appreciations.

Giving needs to be a consistent factor in your relationship. Keep a small notebook with you during the day to record any positive thoughts or feelings you have about your mate. If you really pay attention to the contents of your mind you will notice that many fleeting but pleasant images and thoughts about your partner pop into your head at times when you are doing routine tasks or taking a break from your work. Jot these all down in your notebook and share them at dinner or before sleep every day for a week or two. This will help you develop the habit of expressing your appreciations on a day-to-day basis.

Some people have a "job jar" but a more fun and interesting variation on this is the "giving jar." Individually develop a list of ten or fifteen things you like to give and to get that are free or inexpensive and can be done spontaneously in less than an hour. Some examples from one couple's list are:

Take turns telling each other three reasons why we love each other.

Take turns giving the other a foot or head message.

Go for a walk, holding hands.

Spend five minutes kissing and hugging sensually but not sexually.

Reminisce about how we first met. Tell each other again our first thoughts and feelings about one another.

Tell each other all the ways we think the other is handsome/beautiful and sexy.

Make each other a special handmade card using drawings or magazine pictures that express how we feel about each other.

Turn off all the lights and dance to romantic music.

Bring your lists together and discard any items that are not pleasant to both of you. Write the remaining items on separate slips of paper, fold them and place them in a jar with a wide mouth (a large peanut butter jar is great for this). Once or twice a week pick a slip out of the jar and do the activity. This is a lot more fun than watching TV even when you are tired. When you run out of slips in your giving jar, you can put the same ones back or make up a new set.

Increasing Acceptance in Your Relationship. Set aside a time to discuss your differences. This should be at a time when you are feeling peaceful and relaxed with one another. Define together three differences that you perceive in your relationship. These could be differences in values, feelings, behavior, goals, anything that you are both aware as being a difference between you.

Taking each difference in turn, share with one another your thoughts and feelings about these differences. Make "I" statements rather than "you" statements. For example, saying "I feel very uncomfortable when I am late for an appointment" is more helpful to the process than saying "You are rude and inconsiderate about being on time." Next, working individually, list five good things about your differences and share your list with one another. Now brainstorm together ways in which you can capitalize on the positive aspects of your differences and lessen the impact of the negative aspects.

Finally, sit crosslegged with knees touching, hold hands and make eye contact. Repeat to one another in turn the following phrase until you feel comfortable and centered as you say it:

"I accept you, and I accept our differences."

Once you each feel complete with the above, repeat the following phrase in the same way:

"I accept myself for being different from you."

Some differences are easily resolved and others are more troublesome. You may need several sessions to work through a particularly troublesome one. The forgiveness exercise described earlier is helpful in this process as are the affirmation procedures and the wise man fantasy described in the next chapter.

Building Empathy. The ability to empathize is developed by listening and looking for the feelings a person is expressing through their words and behavior. It means being aware of the tone of voice, the language, and the nonverbal cues your partner is sending you. You can practice building empathy in daily interaction by simply stating what you imagine your partner is feeling at any particular moment and asking if you are right or wrong.

Another way to increase your empathic skills is through a variation on the active listening exercise outlined earlier. In this case, one partner relates an experience they have had some feelings about. It could be a problem at work, an interaction with a friend or relative, or an event from childhood. The content does not matter. Simply tell the story in a natural way. The partner who is the listener responds to the feelings he or she perceives in the narrative. The following is an exerpt from one couple's conversation.

SHE: I remember the day I started my first job. I was walking home after school thinking, "I wonder if I can do it, I wonder if I can do it?"

HE: You must have been pretty nervous.

SHE: Yes, I was really scared, I had no idea what to do or what would happen when I got there.

HE: Were you afraid of embarrassing yourself?

SHE: Yes, I was afraid I'd mess up and that I wouldn't measure up or know how to act. I was pretty self-conscious anyway at that age. But when I got there I was really surprised to find it was so easy.

HE: I'll bet you felt pretty relieved about that.

SHE: I sure did! I even found I enjoyed it most of the time, although it got to be routine after a while.

HE: You must have been bored by the routine.

SHE: Yes, I was . . .

Empathy helps build understanding, trust, and a feeling of being accepted. It encourages people to share themselves and is an important way to give and express caring.

Increasing Sharing in Your Relationship. All of the exercises outlined above enhance sharing. Sharing needs to happen on a regular basis. So many things go on in our busy lives that we can easily lose touch with one another if we do not make an effort to keep each other up to date.

One excellent way to build time for sharing into your regular schedule is the weekly Feelings Meeting. This should take place at the same time each week and is a time just for the two of you to tell one another what has been happening in your respective lives, what you have been thinking about, and how you have been feeling about your life, yourself, and one another. Set aside about two hours for your Feelings Meeting. Many couples do this over a leisurely brunch, a picnic, or while sharing a long walk.

Another way of enhancing sharing is to play the Sharing Game at odd moments. My husband and I do this to turn long and otherwise monotonous drives into a pleasant experience of getting to know one another on ever-deepening levels. Often the Sharing Game turns into a very growthful and interesting discussion. The Sharing Game simply involves taking turns answering a personal question. There is no limit to the questions that can be used in this game. Some examples are:

What was your most embarrassing moment?

When did you first masturbate?

What was the saddest (happiest, most frightening, etc.) experience of your life?

What happened the first time you were away from your parents overnight?

What would you like people to say about you after you die?

Tell me a dream you have had recently.

Where do you see yourself five years from now?

If you could solve any one problem in the world today, what would it be and why?

If you were a food (animal, day of the week, magazine, etc.), which one would you be and why?

Who would you like to change places with?

Use your own creative imagination to come up with more questions for the Sharing Game.

All of the qualities that we have discussed are connected to one another and affect each other. One partner's sharing can be used as an opportunity to build empathic skills and develop more understanding and acceptance by the other. This in turn builds trust and helps both partners feel more caring and an increased willingness to give. Each small act of giving or empathy or acceptance can move the relationship to a new and higher level of intimacy. The closer we become, the more our love will shine out and warm one another. As you try out the various activities in this chapter, you will think of more ways to enhance your joys with one another, your creativity together, and your satisfaction in this area of your life.

11

A Potpourri of Relationship Activities

All of us have deep desires for order, beauty, vitality, adventure, recognition, and love in our lives. Many people today feel blocked in fulfilling these desires, because the alternatives that society seems to offer us do not bring satisfaction. We still feel much the same no matter what cleaning compound, cola, or make of car we choose.

Once we recognize that the source of satisfaction lies within us rather than in our possessions or status in life, then we can begin to view each experience as an opportunity to move toward fulfilling our deepest desires. Reaching out to embrace life and all the feelings we have about it brings us closer to our own true nature as human beings. Partners who wish to share this process with one another will find that life becomes an exciting adventure that is continually enhanced and renewed in their mutual love. The activities in this chapter are a sample of some of the ways that you can unblock your relationship when it loses its momentum and speed up the process of mutual growth that liberates transcendent love.

Relaxing and Energizing. The stresses and tensions of daily life often leave us so exhausted or distracted that it seems we simply do not have the energy to enjoy our times together. Fortunately there are many ways to leave the stress of the day behind. The use of alcohol is one of America's favorite ways of unwinding. However the effect of alcohol on the system, although pleasant in the short run, is ultimately debilitating. Many people have recently discovered exercise to be an excellent method for reducing tension and at the same time increasing healthfulness and a sense of physical well-being. A brisk walk, running, swimming, or a furious game of squash allows you to let out your tensions and frustrations physically instead of holding them inside or anesthetizing them through the use of alcohol or drugs.

The activities that follow are additional ways of relieving stress, reducing tension, and enhancing your energy so that you may enjoy your times together. It is best to do these on an empty stomach or after eating lightly. Try them right after work. You can either tape record the instructions or take turns reading them to one another. Read slowly in a calm and soothing tone of voice. After doing one or two of these activities you will feel ready for a hearty meal, a night out, or a long evening of lovemaking.

Activity one. Find a comfortable spot on a soft rug where you have plenty of room to stretch out on your back. Now close your eyes and take a moment just to experience your body. Where do you feel tense or sore? Do you notice any emotions? Take some time simply to acknowledge how your body feels right now. (Pause ten seconds)

Now raise your arms over your head and stretch the right side of your body. Try to leave the left side totally limp . . . Relax . . . Notice how different the right side of your body feels in comparison to the left. Now stretch the left side, leaving the right side relaxed. Hold it a moment and then let go . . . Lower your arms to your sides. How does your body feel now? (Pause five seconds)

Now begin to pay attention to your breathing. Don't change anything. Just notice how your breath is moving in and out of your nose and lungs. (Pause five seconds)

Now you are going to use your breathing to help you relax your mind. Just let go of all your thoughts and turn your attention to the tip of your nose . . . You may notice that as you breathe in, the tip of your nose feels slightly cool and as you breathe out, it becomes warmer. Take two or three deep breaths and then, breathing normally, concentrate all your attention on the sensations you feel in the tip of your nose. (Pause fifteen seconds)

As you are focusing on the tip of your nose, you may find from time to time that your attention wanders. If that happens, gently bring your awareness back to the tip of your nose. Each breath you take in is filling your body with energy and vitality . . . Each breath you expel is releasing another piece of the tensions of the day. Continue breathing in this manner for a while, allowing each breath to deepen and enhance your sense of well-being and calmness. (Pause three to five minutes)

Now gently bring your attention back to your body lying there comfortably on the floor. Take several deep breaths. Sense the vitality flowing through all of your body. Whenever you are ready, open your eyes and sit up feeling refreshed and alert.

Activity two. Find a comfortable spot on the floor or bed. Lie down on your back, close your eyes, and focus on your breath for a moment or two. (Pause five seconds)

Now take a deep breath and tense every muscle in your body . . . Scrunch up your face, squeeze your toes and feet, tighten your arms, shoulders, chest, pelvis, buttocks, and legs just as much as you can. Hold it . . . hold it . . . Relax. (Pause five seconds)

Now imagine that your body is a hollow shell. Inside the shell you are filled with sticky, syrupy, orange liquid. The liquid fills you from your toes right up to the top of your head . . . Each of your big toes is a faucet. You are going to open the faucets now in your toes and allow this sticky orange fluid to drain out of your body. First open the faucet on your right toe . . . Now open the faucet on your left toe. . . .

You are going to expel the sticky orange fluid by tensing and relaxing each part of your body, one by one. Begin by tensing your right foot . . . Now relax and let the fluid begin to flow out of your toe. Next tense your right shin and calf muscles . . . Relax and feel the orange liquid flowing down and out your big toe . . . Tighten your knees and thigh muscles . . . relax, feeling that sticky orange fluid running right down your leg and out your toe. . . . (Repeat instructions for left leg.) Now tighten your buttocks and pelvis area. Hold it tight and release . . . Next tighten your abdomen and chest pushing down with the muscles in the small of your back . . . Relax, all the while feeling that syrupy orange liquid being expelled down both your legs and out your toes. . . .

Now hunch up your shoulders and tighten your back muscles . . . Release. Make a fist with each hand and tighten your arms . . . Now let go and allow the orange liquid to flow down your body and out your toes. . . .

Next tighten your neck, face, and scalp. Clench your jaws. Squeeze up your eyes. Make a terrible face . . . Release all the orange liquid in your head and neck.

Now just take a moment to experience the feelings in your body. Here and there you will find some places that are still orange and sticky. (Pause five seconds) Imagine there is a hole in the top of your head. Through this hole you are going to pour gallons of cool, sparkling, clear, refreshing water that will circulate all through your body, rinsing out all the remnants of that sticky orange fluid. . . . Begin now to feel the cool, refreshing sensation of that clear sparkling water flowing through you from the top of your head and out your toes, cleansing every part of your body. (Pause thirty seconds)

Now close the hole in the top of your head, let all the water drain out your toes and turn off the faucet in each toe . . . Breathe deeply, allowing each breath to fill your body with clear, bright, glowing light . . . Your body feels light and clean now . . . You are experiencing the glow of healthful well-being. (Pause ten seconds)

Now gently bring your awareness back to the room and whenever you are ready open your eyes, feeling refreshed and alert.

Activity three.   This is a good activity to try after Activity one or two to enhance your vitality and energy even further.

First lie down on the floor in a space where you have plenty of room. Raise your arms over your head and stretch making yourself just as long as you can . . . Release. Now raise and lower each leg in turn just as high as you can, keeping your knee straight and your ankle flexed. Do not point your toes. Do this four or five times for each leg . . . Sit up slowly. Draw your knees up to your chest and clasp your arms around them. Curl your head down to your knees, touching your chin and making yourself into a ball. Now roll back as far as you can go and with enough momentum to allow yourself to return to a sitting position still curled up in a ball. The movement of your body will remind you of a rocking chair. Do this four or five times.

Next stand up straight with your feet about six inches apart. Raise your arms over your head. Stretch them just as far as you can. Keeping your feet on the floor, reach even further, first with your right arm and then with your left as if you are trying to pick a piece of fruit that is just out of reach. Repeat six times.

Now place your feet about eighteen inches apart. Make a fist with each hand and place them on the back of your hips on either side of your spine just below the waist. Flex your knees slightly and lean backwards, relaxing your shoulders and chest. Breathe deeply and hold this position for about thirty seconds. Your legs may begin to tremble. This is just tension being released. Allow the trembling to happen.

Next return to an upright position and allow your head to begin to fall forward slowly and your arms to dangle. Continue to bend forward slowly, relaxing your neck muscles and keeping your knees straight until your hands brush the floor. Just hang there for a few moments and then *slowly* return to an erect posture. Imagine that you are straightening your spine, one vertebra at a time.

Now lie down on your back with your knees raised and your feet flat on the floor as near to your buttocks as possible. Slowly lift your hips off the floor and then continue elevating your back one vertebra at a time until all your weight is resting on your shoulders and feet. Hold this position several seconds and then *slowly* lower your back to the floor, again one vertebra at a time.

Now sit up, legs extended in front of you and knees flat on the floor. Raise your arms over your head and lean forward from the hips as far as you can, keeping your back straight. Drop your hands to your legs, grasping your legs, ankles, or feet, as far forward as you can and gently try to lower your head to your knees. Some people find this very easy and for others it is impossible. Go as far down as you can and relax for a moment there by taking a few deep breaths. Slowly sit up. After doing one or two rounds of these exercises you should be ready for anything.

Sensual Treats. A sensual experience together can be a prelude to sex or simply a nice experience in itself. We all need gentle touching and holding. These needs are even more basic than our sexual needs. Infants who are well fed but not touched and stroked by their caretakers can sicken and even die. As adults we can handle long periods of time without physical stroking. However, the more we take the opportunity to touch and be touched the more we blossom.

Activity one. Set your alarm fifteen minutes earlier than usual. Instead of jumping out of bed and rushing into your day, spend that time holding each other and gently stroking one another's bodies. You do not need to talk. Just enjoy the calm drowsy feeling of your warm bodies close to one another. When it is time to arise, break off your contact with a loving kiss. Just a few brief minutes in each other's arms can make a great difference in how you feel about starting your day.

Activity two. This is a good evening activity that involves all the senses. Before you start, collect a variety of soft fabrics, furs, feathers, etc., that feel luxurious to the skin. Also gather together a selection of bite-size foods of different textures and tastes. Some good examples are cold melon balls, chocolate chips, pieces of shredded wheat crackers, squares of your favorite cheese, banana slices. Be as creative as you like in selecting tastes and textures that are pleasing to you and your mate. You can include a bottle of your favorite wine or some sparkling mineral water to use to clear the palate.

Turn the lights down low. Light some incense and put your favorite soothing music on the phonograph. Create a soft nest on the floor with blankets and pillows. Have the person who will be the receiver remove his or her clothes. As the giver you might want to be nude as well or to wear something brief and sexy.

Now begin stroking the receiver's body with one of the textures you have gathered. Ask what feels good and what tickles or is unpleasant. Pause from time to time to pop a piece of one of the foods into your partner's mouth. Continue this as long as it feels good. Then you can switch positions, the giver becoming the receiver or, if you decide to wait to be the receiver until another evening, finish the activity with a soothing full body massage.

Activity three. Giving a long, slow, gentle massage is one of the nicest things one person can do for another. There are many books and classes available to teach the art of massage. However, even if you know nothing about massage techniques, you and your partner can share the sensory benefits of full-body stroking. The requirements are a quiet place free of distractions and warm enough so that you are comfortable unclothed, some good-smelling lotion, and the two of you. The procedure is simply to slowly and gently apply the lotion to every part of your partner's body, gently stroking the skin until the lotion becomes absorbed. Warm each application of lotion to skin temperature in your hand before applying it to your partner's skin. Take your time and be sure to ask what feels good and what parts of your partner's body need more attention or a more vigorous touch. This activity can be done any time. It is wonderful just before sleep or sex. Your relationship benefits and so does your skin.

Upsetting the Routine.   People who have known each other for a time invariably develop patterns and routines in relating to one another. These are helpful in that they allow people to know what to expect from one another without having to spend time and energy reworking the details of living every day. However, our routines can also develop into boring traps that suck the excitement out of a relationship. Every relationship needs a balance between stability and novelty.

You can analyze together the habits and routines in your relationship to identify the ones that are really helpful and supportive and the ones that have become boring and deadening. If the life has gone out of your evening greeting, change it. If you are both tiring of sex in the same old position, try some new ones, do it in a different room or outside in the open air. If you are weary of the same old foods, experiment together with different combinations of tastes. The following are some suggestions for upsetting the routine and bringing new life into your relationship.

Activity one.   Set aside a weekend in which you will do together all the things you normally do separately. Run your errands, do your chores, and share your relaxation time with one another. While this may be inefficient, it can also be fun and give each of you some insight into the other's life.

Activity two.   Another way to gain insight into your partner's life is to switch roles for a day. Whatever your normal activities of that day, simply trade them. At the end of the day, you can discuss together your feelings about taking on your partner's role, whether it was hard or easy for you, and what you learned about yourselves and one another.

Activity three.   Spend a weekend in a local hotel or one in a nearby city. Be tourists in your own area. This is an especially good activity for people who have children. Leave the children with a sitter or relative. Even if you do not have children, you may be surprised at how much being out of your normal environment will change your experience of one another. Some couples feel rather shy at first when they find themselves alone together in unusual circumstances. Whatever your feelings, if you can discuss them together you will be taking a positive step in enhancing your relationship.

Activity four. Plan your next vacation to go to a place that you have never been and as much as possible is unlike the places you normally go. While on this vacation do as many new and adventurous things together as you can. Try new foods, visit out-of-the-way spots, take a glider flight, go to an amusement park and try the roller coaster, stay up all night together, or get up early for a sunrise walk. Be as creative as you can in thinking of activities to share that you would not normally do.

Sharing Your Path to the Inner Self. People today are becoming increasingly interested in exploring inner space. Who is the "me" that lives in my body and looks out onto the world? How can I release more of my hidden potential and experience a greater sense of unity with all things? What is the meaning of my life? These are all questions that are now being asked by more of us than ever before. It is often assumed that the path to the inner self is a solitary one. The fact is that the more you can share your path with others, the more you will learn about yourself. Couples who are interested in exploring inner space can share their experiences in many ways. The activities that follow are just a few of many possibilities.

Activity one. Sit crosslegged facing one another with knees touching and hands clasped. Take several deep breaths and then make eye contact. Look deep into one another's eyes, noticing any discomfort you feel in your body and monitoring any urge to look away, to smile or laugh, or to break off contact in any way. As soon as you feel centered and comfortable, direct your attention to a spot between your partner's eyes and just above the bridge of the nose. Now allow your eyes to softly unfocus. Hold that position for a while just noticing your own thoughts and being open to your own experience. Do not judge or try to control any of your feelings or sensations. If you find your mind or gaze wandering, gently bring it back to the spot between your partner's eyes. Continue this for ten to fifteen minutes.

Each person's experience of this activity is unique. You may have insights about yourself or your partner; you may have a strong emotional experience; you may feel nothing. Some people have a strong sense of unity with their partner. The experience can vary each time you do this activity. The important thing is to let go of any sense of trying to create an experience and simply to have the experience that you have. After you complete the activity you can share what happened with each other.

Activity two. This activity is a way if dissolving barriers to greater self-expression in your relationship and in your life as a whole. First identify a barrier you would like to overcome. Then form a sentence that states how you will be and feel when you are past that barrier. Suppose, for example, you are experiencing a block in your creativity. The sentence you might use in this activity could be "I am now feeling revitalized by a flood of creative ideas." Or suppose you feel blocked in really expressing your love to your partner. Your sentence in that case might be "I am now able to show my love for _____ freely and spontaneously."

Now sit down facing your partner with knees touching and hands clasped. Make eye contact and repeat your sentence until you can say it without feeling uncomfortable. You may notice that you want to stop, to look away, or that your hands or voice tremble a little as you begin repeating the sentence. Just note these reactions and go on until you can say it firmly and with conviction.

Next have your partner repeat the sentence to you using the form "You are now. . . ." Maintain eye and hand contact and respond after each repetition with the first thought that comes into your head. You may find that your first thoughts are negative ones like "No I can't" or "I doubt it." It does not matter what the thought. Just say it and then listen again as your partner repeats your sentence to you. Continue this process until your first mental responses take on a more positive tone. Then repeat the sentence again to your partner three or four times. Notice your feelings as you do this. Do you feel more or less uncomfortable than you did at first? Finally, switch roles and do the same activity with your partner's sentence.

This is a very powerful activity that can change your life dramatically. It is often helpful to repeat the activity using the same sentence on several consecutive days. The key here is your own feeling of comfort in saying and hearing the words that express how you want to feel and be. The more firm and centered you grow to feel during the activity, the more you will notice changes in your daily experience.

Activity three. Meditation is a technique that has been used for centuries to enable people to get past the level of personality and open the door to awareness of the inner self. Meditating together is a pleasant way to share your inner path and deepen your relationship bond. There are many types of meditation. Use your favorite one or try this activity.

Light a candle and sit comfortably in a place where you can direct your attention to the flame. Allow your eyes to unfocus softly and begin noticing the thoughts, feelings, images, and sensations that pass through your awareness. Label each one and then let it go. If you notice you are hearing a sound, simply say to yourself "hearing" and then open up to your next awareness. When you find yourself thinking of the past just say "memory" and let the thought go. Do the same with whatever sensations you are having as well as the things that you notice in your mind. Some labels you might use are fantasizing, smelling, feeling, worrying, seeing, etc.

At some point you may feel like closing your eyes. It is all right to do this. Just continue the same process with eyes closed. Do this for about twenty minutes. A regular period of meditation once or twice a day is wonderful for clearing the mind, relaxing the body, and opening you to yourself and your relationship.

Activity four. Each of us can be his or her own guru or teacher. We all have depths of knowledge that we rarely tap. This activity is a method for getting in touch with your own inner wisdom. You can do it alone or together. If you are looking for an answer to a relationship problem or a way to be more creative in your relationship together, do this activity jointly to double its power. You can tape record it for this purpose. If one of you has a personal question or an important decision to make, the other can guide you through this activity by reading it aloud. Sometimes you might be aware of feeling stuck but not know what question to ask. In this case simply ask your inner guru "What is the question I need to be asking in my life right now?"

Lie down on your back in a comfortable spot, legs uncrossed and arms at your sides. Pay attention to your breathing for a moment. (Pause ten seconds)

Now imagine you are in a beautiful meadow . . . There are flowers and tall grasses all around you . . . This is the most perfect place you have ever seen . . . There is a slight breeze that ruffles the grass and birds are flying overhead . . . Notice the beautiful cloud formations in the deep blue sky . . . It is very peaceful here, calm and quiet . . . You begin to notice that there is an air of expectancy here as if all of nature were waiting for something to happen. . . . (Pause five seconds)

Notice that across the meadow there is a brook at the edge of a lovely wooded area . . . Now begin walking toward the brook . . . You can hear the sound of the water rushing past as you draw closer. (Pause five seconds)

As you are approaching the brook you see an old bridge that crosses it . . . You take that bridge and cross the stream stepping into the trees . . . Suddenly you recognize this place. It is a magic wood and you realize that this is the home of the Wise Man . . . You sense that he is nearby and now you set off to find him. (Pause fifteen seconds)

When you find the Wise Man, greet him and ask him your question, realizing that he must answer any question put to him by one who has sought him out in his magic wood. (Pause three minutes)

Whenever you are ready now, say good-bye to the Wise Man and retrace your steps out of the magic wood, across the bridge and into the meadow . . . Then come back to this room feeling awake and alive.

By using your personal Wise Man you can think of many more creative activities that will bring you and your partner closer together and open doors to a more joyous experience of one another. The more you focus on loving and sharing together, the more your love will expand and grow.

12

Enlightenment and Intimate Relationships

Enlightenment is one of those words that means many different things to different people. Since there is no material thing called enlightenment (it is not something we can point to or touch), we have a hard time agreeing on its characteristics. In fact, we have a hard time knowing whether or not it is something that truly exists. For some people enlightenment is merely a crazy idea dreamed up by some folks who live far away and prefer to starve to death rather than kill a cow. To others, enlightenment is the purpose and meaning and goal of living. To get an idea of what enlightenment means to you, complete the following sentence five times:

Enlightenment is _____.
Enlightenment is _____.
Enlightenment is _____.
Enlightenment is _____.
Enlightenment is _____.

If you were to describe a pine tree to me and I had only seen maples, we would have trouble agreeing on the real nature of trees. If I had never seen a tree or only seen one once or twice without really knowing what it was, you would have a hard time convincing me that trees exist at all. Unless I knew you very well and trusted your judgment, I would most likely dismiss your arguments and demand that you produce a tree for me to see before I would believe you. If you could not do that I would probably depart, shaking my head over your gullibility and be unlikely to trust your judgment in the future.

So it is with enlightenment. Many people have had an experience of enlightenment, but they are inclined not to discuss it for fear of losing the respect of others. We tend to hide our light from one another and in doing so we undermine our confidence in our own experience. Since few people talk about enlightenment socially and because these experiences are so personal and unique, we often do not recognize an enlightenment experience for what it is. As a result we have some beliefs about enlightenment that may limit us experiencing and understanding it.

The most limiting of these beliefs is that there is no such thing. Enlightenment is simply a concept, a dream, or wishful thinking. Yet enlightenment is an idea that has persisted for many hundreds of years. Countless people down through history have described enlightenment experiences. There is a tradition of mysticism within every major religion, which is usually regarded with wary respect by the more intellectual and moralistic mainstream. In modern times various secular and religious movements have been founded out of the enlightenment experience. Such widely different groups as the Catholic Charismatics, est, and Alcoholics Anonymous are notable examples. Lots and lots of people are writing about enlightenment today whether they call it that or not. The list is endless and ranges from the highly intellectual and secular work of Franklin Merrill-Wolfe to the emotional, pop-religious writings of Jess Lair. There may truly be no such thing as enlightenment, but it is unlikely that these people from different times, lifestyles, and philosophical orientations are talking about an experience that does not exist.

Another belief is that enlightenment, if it does exist, is an experience that only people who withdraw from society have. We have images of the Buddha renouncing his crown and wandering alone in the wilderness, of mystics retreating into celibacy and solitude, of holy men living in mountain caves. These are the people, those who devote their life to meditation, prayer, and seeking the spirit, who get enlightenment after many years of deprivation and hardship. Obviously this is not us. We like good food, comfortable beds, and all the amenities of civilized life. People like us do not experience enlightenment.

When we look again at the enlightenment experiences described in literature it seems that as many fairly ordinary secular people are writing about their enlightenment as hermits and celibates and mystics. Often these ordinary people were not even seeking to be enlightened at the time but were merely going about their business dealing with the hardships of life and trying to make things work. Imagine how many other people must have had similar experiences and never published a book.

Another image we have about enlightenment is that it is a dazzling, dramatic, unusual, once-in-a-lifetime experience that leads to remarkable change in the individual and results in a renunciation of worldly pursuits and a retreat into contemplation. This is like saying the only thing that is a tree is cone shaped and has needles. Obviously some enlightenments are like this. These are the ones we are most likely to hear something about. But they are probably among the most rare. This kind of "Big Bang" enlightenment is just one experience that lies along a continuum of experience. Insight, intuition, creativity, awe, peak experiences, some dreams, some aspects of transcendent love are all experiences that are related to enlightenment. Enlightenment is simply an experience of knowing something you did not know before, of things falling into place, of suddenly having the answers to questions that seemed unanswerable. It is an extremely common experience for most people. The form it takes, the knowledge gained from an enlightenment experience, varies depending on the nature of the questions being asked and the knowledge being sought. I have had at least one enlightenment experience that had to do with cooking. I wanted to enter a recipe contest, and I wanted to win. For several days I posed the question of what would be a winning entry in a contest with these particular rules. In one afternoon the answers popped into my head. First I saw the name of the recipe, then what type of dish it would be and what ingredients to use. Finally, I thought of a description of the dish that I wanted to include with my entry. I made the dish, entered the contest, and won the grand prize. I had never entered a recipe contest before this one or taken a cooking class, nor do I spend much time cooking, although I enjoy it when I do.

Actually, my experience with the recipe contest was a little more dramatic than most everyday enlightenment experiences although not nearly as striking as a "Big Bang" enlightenment. The use of the word enlightenment to describe purely spiritual experiences is a special use of the term. Everyone can look to experiences and find countless examples of small enlightenment occurrences. These can have to do with any subject, from child rearing to how to make big money in business. Take some time right now to jot down three enlightenment experiences you have had, describing what happened and how you felt.

Enlightenment is both a discrete happening and a process—a series of enlightenment experiences leading to a broader and deeper understanding of life. If we recognize that we all have the potential to become enlightened about anything that interests us, then we can acknowledge that enlightenment, in the spiritual sense, is just as available to us as any other kind of enlightenment, if we want it. Answers to questions like: What is the meaning of life? What is my purpose here and how can I lead my life in harmony with my purpose? arise out of posing questions about: What is the meaning of what is going on right now? What is the purpose of my being in this particular situation? and How can I react harmoniously to what is happening currently in my life? Complete the following exercise:

One question I would like to answer is _____.
One question I would like to answer is _____.
One question I would like to answer is _____:
One question I would like to answer is _____.
One question I would like to answer is _____.

Little by little the answers to your particular questions will add up and a general picture specific to your life will emerge. You may find that your enlightenment looks a lot like a beech tree while someone else's that you may have read or heard about seems more like a live oak. It doesn't matter. Trees are trees and enlightenment is enlightenment regardless of how different the particulars.

There is a sense in which we are all already enlightened. We may not recognize it or pay much attention to it but it is still true. The essential self that resides within each one of us, that self that is me or you, is the enlightened part of us. The roles and beliefs we have assumed that keep us from experiencing our essential self are like smoke that has blackened the chimney of an oil lamp. Our light doesn't shine out into the world but it is still there burning merrily. As we remove the layers of belief, assumption and limiting role behavior it is as if we are polishing the dirty lamp. Little by little more of the light can shine through. We feel lighter and we grow more enlightened, more in touch and in tune with true knowledge every day.

Of course, we can smudge up our lamp. We polish it for a while and then neglect it again. Knowing that you are enlightened, having enlightenment experiences and even feeling like an enlightened person do not guarantee that your life will be any different. If I had not sent my prize-winning recipe into the contest before the deadline and in compliance with the contest rules, I never would have won the prize. If I had not had the skills I needed (reading, writing, knowing something about cooking and recipes, shopping, typing, etc.), I could not have won no matter how good my idea was. Actions must be congruent with what we know, and we need to have necessary skills to act harmoniously if we are to be able to translate the knowledge of our essential selves into our daily lives. It does very little good to *know* if we do not also *do.* Knowing is enlightenment; doing is growing toward mastery of life.

When we do begin to act in accordance with our deepest knowings, our lives become immediately and continuously transformed. Small miracles begin to happen. A totally frivolous impulse to enter a cooking contest results in winning a week-long vacation at a fabulous mountain resort. Parking spots begin to appear magically in front of the places we want to go. A coveted job opens up. A long-standing relationship problem dissolves and vanishes. The money needed for a much desired trip abroad suddenly materializes.

Enlightenment is both an instantaneous experience and a life-long process. One of the best things about life is that we never run out of new things to learn. Paradoxically, it is this fact that creates such suspicion about the equally true reality of instant change. We can concentrate on the things left to be learned. The latter will always outweigh the former. But this is the joy rather than the curse of life, for if we knew everything, what would we do with our time? When growth stops, death follows. Not having all the answers is one of the things that keep us alive and is certainly what makes life so interesting. If we see no challenges in life then we quickly become bored and dissatisfied. This is not a fault.

It is simply part of the nature of human life. We can choose to love it or hate it, but we waste time and energy trying to change it.

Most of us would like to have a lot more answers about life than we have right now. When we acknowledge this about ourselves we are acknowledging a desire for enlightenment. *Everyone* wants enlightenment, even those people who do not believe in it. And it is not necessary to believe in it to achieve it, although it is helpful to allow for the possibility. Otherwise, it is difficult to recognize it as it comes and goes in the normal course of daily events.

FINDING A PATH

Seeking enlightenment seems somewhat inappropriate for twentieth-century western people because of the images we have of retiring to caves or monasteries, and renouncing the material world or the satisfactions of relationships with family and friends. It is probably easier in some ways to maintain an enlightenment process away from distractions of bills, sick children, and the hussle-bussle of modern life. Yet modern life has all the qualities necessary for providing an incomparable environment for enlightenment and has the added advantage of allowing many more opportunities to develop the skills needed to exhibit mastery as an enlightened person. Sitting in a cave offers one few chances to see what the effects of new insight and greater understanding might be in the world. The more challenges we confront, the more we can grow in skills and understanding. There are plenty of challenging occupations in today's society. One need only choose the one that seems to fit best in terms of interests, values, and needed skills to find a perfect personal path to enlightenment.

Intimate relationships offer an especially productive path to enlightenment in today's society. The problems we are experiencing in these relationships as we make the transition from utilitarian economic models of relationship to more emotionally and psychologically satisfying forms and experiences are precisely the sort of problems that raise questions of meaning and purpose in life. The delicacy and fragility of the bonds between partners reflects the sensitivity of these relationships to the presence or lack of growth. It is easy to see how well you are doing on your path by the well-being and love you and your partner are experiencing and by the sense of movement or lack of movement toward resolution of interpersonal conflicts. In order to make a relationship work, those issues that prevent one from having a sense of the essential self must be transcended. Inhibiting roles and beliefs are challenged by intimate relationships far more strongly than in any other area of life. The feelings of love and excitement are quickly extinguished if we are not moving toward greater clarity and understanding of ourselves and our relationship with life. Therefore, the state of our intimate relationships provides a source of immediate feedback on how we are doing on our path toward enlightenment.

How to do it, of course, is the next question which occurs to us. Actually, this whole book is as much a handbook for enlightenment as it is a new way of looking at love relationships. By focusing attention on discovering and implementing ways that work to get the joy and love that we deeply desire from our relationships, we will be naturally enlightening our lives. The more we can allow our light to shine with those closest to us, the more support and information we will have for shining in the outside world as well.

We live in exciting times. The same technology that brought us atomic weaponry, pollution, and worldwide Coca-Cola has also given us longer life spans, increased leisure time, and a measure of intellectual and emotional freedom never before available to large masses of people. If we want to understand the nature of human existence, we first need to understand our own nature. If we wish to know how to bring peace and harmony into the world, we can first learn to create harmonious interactions with those closest to us. Should we want to change the world, the first step is to transform our own lives.

One person's effort can make a difference. I sat in on a meeting recently where one person in a subsidiary position was beginning to transform a long-standing situation characterized by apathy and disinterest. He did this by simply saying what was on his mind in a skillful and diplomatic way. Judging from the instantaneous positive and cooperative responses from the rest of the group, it seemed almost as if they had been waiting for something like this to happen. The results were an immediate transformation from a group of bored and lethargic people to a vital and creative team commited to changing their program from "good enough" to excellent.

Everyone's life touches the lives of countless other individuals. One person does make a difference, a truly incalculable one. Regardless of your position in life, you have the opportunity to change the world. To do this, you need to do your homework. No change that does not come out of being true to one's deepest self will hold the truth that is desperately needed in today's world. It does not matter if your goal is to win a recipe contest or to solve the problem of world hunger. The process is exactly the same and your impact on the world will be just as important.

Each person's path is defined by the questions he or she is asking of life. How can I help my child with his problems? How can I respond to my husband's need? How should I handle the situation at work? Where can I best use my talents right now? What do I have to offer? When we ask ourselves questions like these we are shaping our lives and creating the contexts in which our growth process can take place.

Setting one's path is very nice. The important thing, however, is to take each step along it. The first step for all of us is to handle the immediate issues in our personal lives. There is no way to skip over an issue constructively. To handle it may mean leaving it, changing it, or coming to terms with our own resistance to it. It does not mean running away from it. Skipping over is often a temptation for all of us. But to do so leaves us without the skills we will need for our next step and with energy tied up in unfinished business.

Actually, it is very unusual to be able to see more of one's path than the next step or two along the way. The secret of enlightenment is in finding the joy in responding to each situation that life brings us with all of the strength and love that we are able and in knowing that we will never really be finished. As a goal, enlightenment is elusive. At the same time it is compelling and absorbing. Relationship partners who can learn to support one another along the way will reap the rewards of endless excitement and ever-deepening love.

Index